MERRILL·C·TENNEY

12 QUESTIONS JESUS ASKED

This book is designed for your personal reading pleasure and profit. It is also designed for group study. A leader's guide with helps and hints for teachers and visual aids (Victor Multiuse Transparency Masters) is available from your local bookstore or from the publisher.

VICTOR BOOKS

a division of SP Publications, Inc.
WHEATON ILLINOIS 60187

Offices also in Fullerton. California • Whitby. Ontario. Canada • Amersham-on-the-Hill. Bucks. England

Recommended Dewey Decimal Classification: 232
  Suggested Subject Heading: CHRISTOLOGY

Library of Congress Catalog Card Number: 81-50767
  ISBN: 0-88207-346-x

©1980 by SP Publications, Inc. All rights reserved
Printed in the United States of America

VICTOR BOOKS
A division of SP Publications, Inc.
P.O. Box 1825 • Wheaton, Illinois 60187

TO MY GRANDDAUGHTERS
MARY AND JANET
WHO WILL HAVE TO ANSWER
THE QUESTIONS THAT
JESUS ASKED

Contents

Introduction

The use of questions characterized all of Jesus' teaching. From the beginning of His ministry to its end He was continually probing the minds and memories of His hearers. These questions were not academic, but personal. His aim was not to gain information for Himself, but to stimulate discussion with others, and to bring them to a commitment to Himself and to His program. He used this method to compel consideration of His claims, and to draw from His disciples the confession that would seal their allegiance to Him.

The selection of questions in this book shows how He dealt with these major issues of life that still concern men vitally: the need of belonging to someone or something, the governing factor of their choices, the problem of fear, and others. Jesus discussed these in a way that appeals to one's sense of responsibility, while at the same time presenting His sufficiency for their needs. The principles which He taught by interrogation are perennially applicable, and are particularly relevant to the stress of modern times.

Thanks are due to the editorial staff of Victor Books for cheerful encouragement and wise counsel.

Merrill C. Tenney
Wheaton, Illinois
May 1980

1
Where Do I Belong?

"How is it that ye sought Me? Knew ye not that I must be in My Father's house?"   Luke 2:49, ASV

The Feast of Passover had ended, and the pilgrims were making their way home from Jerusalem as rapidly as possible. The road northward toward Galilee was crowded with tired adults, chattering children, and braying donkeys who protested their reluctance at being hurried through the afternoon heat of a spring day. Everyone was physically and emotionally drained by the excitement and tensions of the feast. As the sun declined in the west and the afternoon shadows lengthened, the travelers reached a camping site and began to settle down for the night.

On this particular occasion, Mary and Joseph had taken Jesus up to Jerusalem for His introduction to the temple. He was 12 years old, the age at which the Jewish boy became *bar mitzvah*, "a son of the Law," and was admitted to the adult community of the synagogue. For Jesus the trip must have been doubly meaningful: He would, possibly for the first time, have seen the great temple and shared in the mysterious and awesome ritual of its worship. And He would also have been inducted into the company of believing Israel as a member in His own right. Whether or not He had previously visited Jerusalem when Joseph and Mary annually made the pilgrimage, this occasion was a most memorable one.

As the Galilean neighbors arrived at the camp, each family began to gather in its own place. Along the road the children liked to travel with their friends, and frequently were not in the company of their immediate families. When Joseph and Mary looked for Jesus, He was missing. Immediately they questioned their neighbors to see if He had strayed into another group. Apparently nobody had seen Him since the cavalcade left Jerusalem, nor did anyone have a suggestion as to where He might be found.

Wearily, Joseph and Mary retraced their steps to Jerusalem and renewed their search there, but with no immediate result. Finally, after three days of combing the lodging places, alleys, and bazaars of the city, they found Him in the temple, listening to the theological discussions of the teachers of the law, and asking them questions. Apparently He had been questioned also, for the text states that the hearers were astonished at the aptness of His answers.

When Joseph and Mary entered the court and saw Him, they could not restrain themselves. Their apprehensiveness was obviously relieved when they realized that He was safe, but the strain of the protracted uncertainty prompted them to remonstrate with Him: "Son, why hast Thou thus dealt with us? Behold, Thy father and I have sought Thee, sorrowing" (Luke 2:48).

His rejoinder to them contains the initial question of a dedicated life: "How is it that ye sought Me? Knew ye not that I must be about My Father's business?"

A Question of Commitment

This question was not an impertinence, but the logical inquiry of one who has committed himself to God. Joseph and Mary had brought Jesus to Jerusalem for the express purpose of involving Him in the temple worship. The Hebrews depended greatly on representative faith. Families worshiped as a unit, and the ritual experience became the evidence of reality. Since they had introduced Jesus to the temple and thus confirmed His dedication, they were responsible for establishing His relation to God.

Now Jesus expressed surprise that they had not realized His imperative obligation to His Father, God. He felt a close tie to the temple, for it was the place where God's presence was peculiarly real and where, consequently, Jesus belonged. He may not at this time have been fully aware of His origin, though it is not at all unlikely that concurrently with His reaching the age of moral maturity, Mary or Joseph would have informed Him. In any case, He was conscious of a special relation to the God to whose worship He was devoted.

There was, of course, no rebellion against Mary and Joseph in whose home He had been nurtured. Luke states that "He went down with them, and came to Nazareth, and was subject unto them" (Luke 2:51). As far as His human relations were concerned, He was a normal Jewish boy who honored His father and mother, and dutifully submitted to their training.

Jesus' question, however, carries some other overtones. One relates to the small word *must* that occurs in it. This term implies not simply an obligation contracted by chance, but the inevitability of inherent design. A triangle *must* have three sides, not because it has agreed to accept that condition, but because otherwise it would not be a triangle. A stone that loosens from a cliff *must* fall, not because of any choice that it can exercise, but because it is subject to the law of gravity. When Jesus attained the age at which His choice for God was declared, He belonged to His Father's house, and would logically be expected to be there.

This term *must* appears frequently in the speech of Jesus. In the Gospel of Luke alone, it occurs nine other times. He used it concerning His mission of preaching the kingdom of God (4:43), concerning the visit to Zaccheus' house (19:5), concerning the necessity of His suffering and death (9:22; 13:33; 17:25), and concerning the fulfillment of Scripture (22:37; 24:7, 26, 44). In the Gospel of John, the word *must* refers to Jesus' passage through Samaria (4:4), to His healing of a blind man (9:4), to His mission to Gentiles (10:16), to His vicarious death (12:34), and to the fulfillment of prophecy (20:9). It indicates that Jesus lived all His life under an imperative, which was not a fatalistic imposition of an unwelcome destiny, but the program of action on which He and the Father had agreed. His career had been declared in the Scriptures written before His appearance on earth, and was carried out according to the plan and purpose of God.

This appearance in the temple was the first acknowledgment of His allegiance to the will of God. The Father's desire was the rule of His life and took precedence over everything else. His presence in the temple demonstrated the nature of His intellectual interests and emotional attachments, and the priorities of His choices. God's house, God's work, and God's plan came first.

Relationship to His Father

A second implication of this text is Jesus' consciousness of God. Luke informs us that Jesus was "subject unto" Joseph and Mary, that He returned with them to Nazareth, and that He "increased in wisdom and stature, and in favor with God and man" (2:51-52). He had a normal development as a boy; and as He grew to manhood, there came advancing maturity, such as would appear in anyone. He was in no sense a precocious freak. Yet the normal development contained an increasing sense of the reality of God as His Father. To Him, God was not a distant and terrible deity, whom He worshiped from afar and whose existence was accepted only as part of religious training. Throughout His life He invariably spoke of God as His Father, and often indicated that He maintained with God a close and constant fellowship. The affiliation was so close that Jesus was always aware of the Father's presence and keenly sensitive to the Father's will. When explaining to Philip the reality of God, Jesus said: "Believest thou not that I am in the Father, and the Father in Me?" (John 14:10)

This relationship was basically spiritual. Another episode recorded by Mark defines this fact more plainly. On one occasion, while Jesus was preaching to a large crowd, His mother and brothers came to see Him, and summoned Him by a messenger. The crowd, realizing that He was wanted, interrupted Him to tell him so. Looking around Him, Jesus said, "Who is My mother, or My brethren? . . . Whosoever shall do the will of God, the same is My brother, and My sister, and mother" (Mark 3:31-35). Awareness of the presence of God is directly connected with doing the will of God. A life that is controlled by God's governing purpose is sure to feel the confidence that grows from acquaintance with Him.

A Dual Relationship

Jesus, therefore, had a double obligation, first to the Father, who was the origin of His life and for whose purpose He became incarnate; and secondly to the family into which He was born and with whom He sustained normal human relations. The former relation was not a myth; for Jesus it was a supreme reality. The latter relation could not be set aside lightly because of the supreme importance of the former. Jesus maintained connections with His brothers; and even at the cross, He made provision for the care of His mother. His position as the Son and Messenger of God was His prime concern; yet it included the discharge of all the responsibilities that are inherent to membership in the human race. His unswerving devotion to the will of the Father and His loyalty to His family and friends were parallel, not contrary.

This dual relationship of Jesus to His heavenly Father and to the family into which He was born is duplicated in the lives of believers. We each find within ourselves an awareness of the reality of God, for "whosoever believeth that Jesus is the Christ is born of God" (1 John 5:1). At the same time, we are aware of our membership in the human race because we belong to it by natural birth. We have a vertical relationship to God and a horizontal relationship to our fellowmen.

A Growing God-Consciousness

The consciousness of this double relationship seems to have grown with Jesus as He progressed from childhood to adulthood. The initial question was elicited by worried parents who were delighted to discover Him unharmed, but whose ill-concealed alarm at His absence implied reproach. He was declaring His main objective in life, to "dwell in the house of the Lord forever" (Ps. 23:6). He wanted them to understand that as He came to maturity, He belonged chiefly to God, and His career must be regulated by divine command.

However, He never used this as an excuse for rebellion or neglect. Tradition suggests that Joseph died before Jesus began His preaching, and that Jesus assumed the financial responsibility for the family.

Be that as it may, it does seem that His consciousness of the plan of God for His life was ever widening. Luke indicates that the knowledge of His place in the prophetic pattern of Scripture appeared in the first public utterance at Nazareth: "Today hath this Scripture been fulfilled" (Luke 4:21, ASV). As He continued in His ministry, He declared the necessity of enlarging His borders, for He said, "I must preach the kingdom of God to the other cities also; for therefore was I sent" (4:43, ASV). That ministry was expanded not only geographically, but also to the irreligious as well as to the religious, for He said, "I am not come to call the righteous, but sinners to repentance" (5:32, ASV). The last year of His life evoked the repeated predictions that He must suffer a fate that would to the Jewish mind exclude Him from Messiahship and that would brand Him as a failure. The resolution to go to Jerusalem (9:51) was the determination to carry out this part of His mission (18:31-33). This progression of awareness, in Jesus' realization of these stages, does not imply His ignorance of them in advance. More likely it shows that He did not discuss the unfolding scenes with His disciples until the time called for the disclosure.

Citizenship in Two Worlds

For Jesus and for each of us, two worlds of differing character and principle present their claims. As children of God, "in Him we live, and move, and have our being" (Acts 17:28). He has a right to demand our primary allegiance; as the psalmist says: "It is He who hath made us . . . we are His people" (Ps. 100:3). If we claim Him as our Father, we are bound to acknowledge our sonship. As members of the family of God, we must remember that the privilege carries duties with it.

1. *The kingdom of God.* Membership in the family of God implies that we should make the family circle our headquarters. Christians are not to be snobbish in the sense that they refuse to associate with anybody else, or show no interest in those who do not share their faith. Yet their primary obligation is to each other, for within the family circle lies their true home. In sorrow, they have comfort; in danger, protection; in joy, true understanding; when threatened, a common defense. The Father's house provides a place where fellowship

should always be available, and a society in which each has a responsibility to discharge.

Within the Father's house, there is a common sense of purpose and a shared objective to be attained. It is like a family business in which all members have an interest. Some are manufacturers who produce the goods for market. Some are salesmen who present the produce to the world. Some are accountants who manage the financing of the business. God Himself is the Head of the household who decides the policies of the entire enterprise (Eph. 4:6).

Membership in this household determines the attitudes toward each other. To belong to the family of God makes all believers brothers and sisters, and establishes a standard by which conduct and concern should be measured. In dealing with the consequent care for each other, the Scriptures admonish us not to put a stumbling block in the way of the brother for whom Christ died (Rom. 14:13, 15). The family of God is an unbreakable unit in which quarrelsomeness, slander, envy, and rivalry have no place. Kindness, cooperation, and mutual aid are enjoined upon us. All of us have set before us the model of "the measure of the stature of the fullness of Christ" (Eph. 4:13), which can be attained only when all are aiding each other toward the same goal.

Jesus' relationship with the Father kept Him from sinning. His interests lay in the domain of God, not in experimentation with evil. His early presence in the temple revealed that the entire trend of His life was toward righteousness. The maintenance of constant contact with God develops a consciousness that separates men from sin.

Our family once employed a man from the Salvation Army who was a skilled painter. He had been a seafaring man; and like many who spend long lonely hours away from home, he had become an alcoholic. He remarked that when he was at home with his family, he seldom wanted to drink because of the effect it would have on his son. But when he was separated from his family, the temptation became irresistible. The family relationship was a deterrent to what he knew to be injurious. Remembering that we are related to God and living in His presence are often sufficient to keep us from harmful laxity and disobedience.

Jesus' place in the house of God put Him in the society where God's truth was discussed and studied. As a normal boy, He learned from the things that He heard and saw. The divine intelligence He possessed was growing in human surroundings. The teachers of the law, even though they were often bound by tradition, were nevertheless learned men who had a deep reverence for God's truth. As Jesus listened to the teachers, He learned their arguments and how to understand their thinking.

2. *The society of mankind.* Jesus was also a member of this present world of time and space. Like Jesus, we too belong to the here and now. We can neither crawl back into the past nor withhold action until some future date when circumstances will seem more favorable for us. We cannot avoid the responsibilities which the present entails. Jesus did not seek to avoid them. Rather He solved the problems of the present by applying to them the eternal principles of the will of God.

According to the Scriptures, we have a dual citizenship. We are citizens of the kingdom of God, and yet we are members of the society into which we were born. As citizens of the kingdom of God, we are eligible for its privileges and are bound by its laws. As citizens of society, we are strangers and pilgrims (Heb. 11:13), traveling through a land whose inhabitants do not seek a destination farther ahead of them.

Our Christian destiny gives us a different perspective! Life here on earth is transient, but not trivial, for it is the proving ground in which we demonstrate the meaning of our heavenly calling and the reality of our knowledge of God. Just as a tourist desires to give a good impression of his native country by his exemplary behavior in the place which he visits, so the Christian pilgrim wishes to exhibit to the world the glory of the kingdom to which he belongs and to which he is returning. Jesus asserted frequently that He came down from heaven (John 3:13, 31; 6:38, 42; 8:23; 17:14), and He demonstrated the quality of His heavenly citizenship by His life on earth. He avowed also that His objective in returning to the Father's house was to prepare a place for His disciples (John 14:3). The temple was for Him only the emblem of the real temple above, the presence of God. There is the eternal abode of God's people—a place where no structure is needed because God's presence is so pervasive that it fills all things and surrounds all people with His nearness.

There is, therefore, a certain detachment that characterizes every Christian. He has loyalties to his family, to his friends, to his business associates, and to his country, that ought to be sustained. But they are at best temporary, for death sunders him from his possessions, his surroundings, and his contemporaries. To make these the principal focus of his affections is to invite futility. These loyalties are not valueless, nor are they to be despised. But neither are they permanent. Abiding trust can be placed only in "the Father's house."

One of my friends once told how he was called to the bedside of a dying man with whom he had been only slightly acquainted. He had never considered him to be a believer, and was rather surprised that he had been summoned to minister to him. When he entered into the bedchamber, he found the man reclining on a pillow, and failing rapidly. Some word of hope was needed, but there was no time for lengthy counsel. How could he communicate the Gospel effectively at that moment? As he looked at the man, he observed that he held clutched in his hand a large roll of bills, as if he were relying on them to provide his security. Over the head of the bed was a crucifix. Taking the roll of money from the fingers, my friend placed in them the crucifix instead and pointed to the figure of Christ, hoping that the gesture might convey a message that words could not transmit. The man's tense muscles relaxed. His eyes showed a gleam of acceptance, and over his face stole an expression of assent and peace. In a few seconds he was gone, but as far as could be ascertained from his silent response, he had reached out in faith to the Lord Jesus Christ, and entered into the Father's house.

"Blessed are the dead who die in the Lord." But how much more blessed are they who live all their lives in the Father's house, doing the Father's business. It is the only place where man can find his real center for living. In every other environment the Christian believer is an alien; in the presence of God he finds his true home. Thus the city of God will be our final destination, where there is no temple, "for the Lord God Almighty and the Lamb are the temple of it" (Rev. 21:22).

2
Who's Boss?

"Why call ye Me Lord, Lord, and do not the things which I say?"
Luke 6:46

The Sermon on the Mount is a very disturbing and revolutionary document. Jesus was not engaged in the business of soothing suburbanites. Rather, He was attempting to penetrate the illusions of His day with the strong realities of the kingdom of God. He pronounced blessings on the poor, the hungry, the rejected, and the persecuted, who were generally regarded as negligible. He made such radical statements as "Love your enemies," and "Lay not up for yourselves treasures on earth" (Matt. 5:44; 6:19).

As His disciples listened to Him, they must have wondered whether such contradiction of the ordinary ethic of life could be practical. Jesus, however, was serious; and at the conclusion of His presentation, He challenged them: In the moral choices of life, whose authority would they recognize—His, or another's? If they professed to recognize His lordship, why did they not follow His injunctions?

The answer to this question calls instantly for a settlement of *the meaning of lordship.* "Lord" is the English translation of the Greek *kyrios,* which might denote the master of a slave or the ruler of a household. It could be merely a title, and is still so used in modern Greek as a polite greeting, *Kalemera, Kyrie!* or, "Good morning, Sir!"

In some contexts of Jesus' time, it was a title of deity. There still survives an ancient letter of a young adventurer who had enlisted in the marines and was shipped to Rome for training. Upon his arrival he wrote a note to his father in which he remarked, "I thank the Lord Serapis, that when I was in danger on the sea, he saved me." Serapis was an Egyptian god worshiped in many parts of the Roman Empire. The title *Kyrios* was used to ascribe deity to him. Later, in the period of the imperial persecutions, Christians were commanded to sprinkle a pinch of salt on the altar of the emperor and to say, "Kyrios Kaisar," or "Caesar is Lord." By so doing they would renounce Christ and would acknowledge the deity of the emperor.

In the context of Jesus' question, He was asking these men why they should call Him *Master* if they did not intend to obey Him. A reconsideration of their relationship was in order. Either they must give up all pretense to discipleship or validate their profession by their actions. Jesus would not accept a halfhearted attachment which could be ended at any time. As their Teacher, He expected the disciples to accept His authority as greater than their own. Christ possessed a heavenly wisdom that far exceeded theirs. He was much more thoroughly versed in the Scriptures than were the fishermen, whose acquaintance with the Old Testament was somewhat desultory. He was able to interpret the Law and the Prophets with the assurance of One who knew their background and who embodied their spirit. The disciples recognized His spiritual ascendancy over them.

When they became Christ's disciples, they accepted Him as the Lord over their lives. They followed His leadership and traveled with Him wherever He went. They did not always understand Him, but they were ready to undertake any risk to which He was exposed, and openly confessed that they would willingly lay down their lives for Him (John 11:15-16; 13:37). Their sincerity was obvious, but their motivation was untried; and when the crisis occurred, they did not fulfill their promises.

They even worshiped Him, for Peter declared, "Thou art that Christ, the Son of the living God" (John 6:69). In placing Jesus above the Law and the Prophets, Peter was expressing his realization that he owed a higher allegiance to Jesus than the ordinary loyalty a disciple shows for his teacher.

Jesus, however, was not satisfied. He demanded more than applause and approval. The requirement of lordship is *obedience* to the authority of Christ. There can be no halfway consent to His commands. Either Jesus is Lord of all areas of life, or the ascription of lordship to Him is meaningless.

Areas of Obedience to the Lordship of Christ

Obedience influences your *career*. Jesus began by summoning these men from their fishing nets to serve Him. When Jesus saw Simon Peter and Andrew plying their trade by the seaside, He said to them, "Come ye after Me, and I will make you to become fishers of men" (Mark 1:17, ASV). Promptly, they left their nets and boats, and accompanied Him on the long itinerary that led through Galilee and Jerusalem and back to the familiar hills in their own territory. Yet when they were disappointed and disillusioned by His death, and had returned to their fishing, Jesus had to renew His challenge (John 21). He was insistent that they should love Him more than they loved the life to which they were accustomed. Fishing was not a sinful occupation, but it was not what He had chosen for them. His service came first, and obedience should determine their occupation.

About 50 years ago, I knew a young man from a Christian home, who chose a career in law. After graduation from law school, he established a thriving practice. He was about to be appointed to a judge's bench when God summoned him to the ministry. After a struggle he surrendered to Christ, entered the ministry, and became a successful pastor and evangelist. Although it was not easy for him to abandon what had begun as a promising career in the legal and political field, Christ took precedence over all other claims.

To obey Christ in your career does not necessarily imply the professional ministry, as if that were the only way of fulfilling His will. Any occupation can be His service, if He so directs. Whether you become a missionary, a lawyer, or a farmer is not the test of obedience. The basic question is, *Who selects the career?* Since Christ is the Lord of the harvest, He has the right to place you in the most strategic position. Only by accepting the place of His choosing can you be sure that your life will be fruitful, whether you become prominent or obscure. Jesus called His disciples to His service, and He insisted that they should never deviate from the course that He had marked for them.

Obedience affects your *emotions.* Jesus commanded His disciples to love their enemies. Such an attitude seems impossible when one considers how crafty, implacable, and cruel enemies can be. Negative reaction to enmity is instinctive; the natural alternative is to fight or to flee, but not to love. Nevertheless, Jesus commanded the impossible, and exemplified it Himself. He indulged in no harsh accusations against the council that condemned Him unjustly; He did not wither Pontius Pilate by a scathing denunciation of his cowardice and failure to observe the rules of Roman justice; nor did He curse the brutal soldiers who nailed Him to the cross. On the contrary, He endeavored to win Pilate to the truth which He embodied, and prayed for those who executed Him.

Bishop Festo Kivengere of Kenya was hounded out of his country by Idi Amin. The bishop narrowly escaped by traveling over back roads at night until he reached the border and crossed into another country. After living in exile for two years, he returned to aid in rebuilding a shattered nation and a bleeding church. In the meantime he published a book entitled *I Love Idi Amin* (Spire), in which he expressed his concern for his enemy, and voiced his prayer for the man's salvation. In his emotional attitude, Festo Kivengere obeyed Christ literally. Lordship affects not only acts, but attitudes as well.

Obedience changes your *prayers*. Jesus Himself is the prime example of this principle. At the end of His career, having fulfilled the public work that He was sent to accomplish, He faced consciously the prospect of a grim and humiliating death. He could have averted it by fleeing across the Jordan and beyond the immediate reach of the Jewish Sanhedrin and the Roman prefect. Instead, He knelt in prayer, waiting for the arrival of His captors, and asking only that the will of His Father be done. His prayers were governed completely by the plan of God. As the divine purpose was progressively revealed, He followed it step by step until the final crisis came. Even then He pressed forward, believing that God would preserve Him through death. His complete trust is the model for your obedience of His lordship in your prayers.

Obedience releases your *possessions*. Your property is not your own. It is a stewardship which has been entrusted to you to administer as God directs, and not in conformity with selfish whims. The possession of wealth is not in itself wrong. It does seem that God has given to some the opportunity to gain property and to administer it. But the use of financial assets for self-gratification and ostentation is a sin. Jesus said: "Lay not up for yourselves treasures upon the earth, where moth and rust consume, and where thieves break through and steal; but lay up for yourselves treasures in heaven, where neither moth nor rust doth consume, and where thieves do not break through nor steal; for where thy treasure is, there will thy heart be also" (Matt. 6:19-21, ASV). Investments in the bank of heaven can never be plundered, embezzled, or mismanaged. They pay dividends that can go on forever.

When Dr. Akira Hatori was a young man, he was led to Christ by a missionary who helped to educate him and to aid him in preparing for the ministry. He was bright and promising, and soon exhausted all the educational resources available for him in Japan. Realizing that he could not earn enough money there to pursue studies elsewhere, the missionary gave him her meager savings and sent him to America for further training. She invested time, money, and prayer in him, believing that God would use him as a voice to his own people. Today, he is one of the outstanding Christian leaders in Japan, a land in which evangelical Christians comprise less that one percent of the population.

Such wise investment springs from the acceptance of the lordship of Christ over possessions. When Jesus commented on the wealthy young aristocrat who had refused discipleship—remarking that rich men could enter the kingdom of God only with difficulty—Peter reminded Him that he and the other disciples had left all to follow Him, and asked what their reward would be. The question revealed that Peter was still thinking of what he would obtain from Jesus, rather than of how he could serve Him. He had not caught the idea that the service of Christ would be prompted by love rather than by gain.

Obedience purifies your *choices*. The major problem of choice for a Christian is not between what is good and evil. There the difference is clearly marked by the Word of God, and leaves no room for hesitation. Redemption commits you irrevocably to the abandonment of evil and to the pursuit of righteousness.

The real problem is the choice between what is good and what is best. There are many options that are apparently equally allowable and beneficial to all concerned, yet which are mutually exclusive. There is opportunity for one only, not for both. If both are permissible, is it a matter of indifference which you shall choose? Shall you take the one which is seemingly more advantageous for you?

The answer lies in the priority of the will of God. Only He can see life from the perspective of eternity and so guide your destiny that it will have eternal significance. The difference between the good and the best is that the good is innocuous but temporary; the best is constructive and eternal. The good may provide necessary staging; the best becomes part of the enduring structure.

Reasons for Obedience to the Lordship of Christ

The lordship of Christ is really a question of management. Who controls your life? Is it Christ? A business will thrive or fail, depending on the quality of the management. If an expert directs it, it will prosper; if the proprietor is unskilled or negligent or extravagant, bankruptcy is the inevitable result.

Life is a complicated business, and must be managed by an expert. No human being is competent to manage his own life successfully, for he has not lived long enough to experience life as a whole. Until he has that experience, he will make all kinds of blunders which will prove damaging, if not fatal. By the time that he has acquired the necessary experience to live prudently, the most productive period of his career will have passed. He is confronted with the dilemma of making mistakes through inexperience, and of having too short a time after the experience is acquired to enjoy his competence. He needs the advice of an expert from the very beginning.

Jesus is such an expert. He encountered every major problem that life can present. He was experienced in *temptation*. At the very outset of His ministry, He was tested by the devil. Alone in the barren wilds of the Judean wilderness, He endured the pangs of hunger, the privation of loneliness, the desire for power, and the allurements of sudden fame. Satan suggested that Jesus take a shortcut to attaining His kingdom, but He sternly refused. While He could have reasoned that the end would justify the means, He would not take any secondary method of accomplishing the work which had been entrusted to Him. Yielding to the temptations would not have infringed any moral code, but would have been a violation of His relationship to His Father. "For in that He Himself hath suffered being tempted, He is able to help them that are tempted" (Heb. 2:18).

Jesus' expertise in meeting all varieties of temptation is needed in the management of life. He can analyze the nature of each temptation from the standpoint of its potential consequences, as well as by its immediate spiritual peril. The most dangerous temptations that a Christian faces are not those that involve a sudden loss of moral integrity. In the most treacherous temptations, Satan tries subtly to deflect the Christian from the intention of God for his life. A believer's protection in these hairline decisions is the lordship of Christ.

Jesus understands the pressures of *service*. When the treachery of a trusted colleague tends to make us sour or cynical, or when disappointments in professional or business life upset us, we can recall that Jesus was denied by one apostle, betrayed by another, and deserted by most of them. Nevertheless, He did not accuse God of injustice nor abandon His calling as being futile and unprofitable. He can instill confidence into the disillusioned. He can heal the wounds of broken promises and deliberate betrayals. He encourages us to persist in the task which God has given us to perform, even though others fail us or obstruct our way.

Jesus is able to cope with the *pressures of poverty*. He never owned His own home. His transportation consisted of His feet, never a chariot. When He wanted a coin for an illustration, He had to borrow it. If He needed a pulpit, a fishing boat served His purpose. He did not even own a grave, and His was provided by Joseph of Arimathea. All through His ministry, He was dependent on others for support; and when He did have some money, it was His habit to give it to the poor.

Jesus can still provide bread for the hungry, shelter for the homeless, and work for the unemployed. "Though He was rich, yet for your sakes He became poor, that ye through His poverty might become rich" (2 Cor. 8:9, ASV). As Lord of our fortunes, He is able to exalt those who are deprived and humble over those who are self-satisfied and arrogant.

Because He is Lord of our fortunes, He can save us from *frustration*. When we labor to accomplish some purpose and fail, we may feel depressed and discouraged. Sometimes this occurs because we have selected the wrong objective. When Christ shapes our lives, He destines us for ultimate success. He is not in the business of making failures.

Failure should not be equated with obscurity. The success of a life does not depend on spectacular effects or on publicity, but rather on total obedience. The design of God is not always immediately apparent. When Jesus died, the witnesses believed that His influence had ended and that His cause was extinguished. He Himself cried out, "My God, My God, why hast Thou forsaken Me?" (Mark 15:34) Nevertheless, God by Christ's death accomplished the redemption of a world, and made the lonely execution on Calvary the pivot of the ages.

When everything seems to go wrong, when cherished hopes are unfulfilled and the work of a lifetime totters on the verge of collapse, then confidence in the lordship of Christ is the antidote to frustration. In the perspective of eternity, He is working out what we see only partially in time.

When an Oriental weaver undertakes to produce a rug, he places the yarn on the loom, and then proceeds to weave a pattern. Anybody looking at the weaving from the back of the loom sees only a mass of knotted tufts of various colors that have neither design nor beauty. We might wonder whether the weaver has any purpose or sense in his work. Upon the completion of the rug, when viewed from the weaver's side, the real beauty and design are perceptible. We usually see life from the wrong side, and feel that it is a mass of inexplicable confusion, random choices, and gross mistakes. But when God's work is finished, the pattern will appear, and it will be perfect.

Similarly the lordship of Christ gives strength for *opposition*. "Be of good cheer," He said. "I have overcome the world" (John 16:33). Opposition of one kind or another always confronts Christians. It may come from people, from circumstances, or from our own nature. Yet in obedience we can say, "I can do all things in Him that strengtheneth me" (Phil. 4:13, ASV). Christ can enable us to resist attack, to circumvent subtlety, to expose deceit, and to win victories by following His directions.

The lordship of Christ avails in the hour of *death*. When we are parted from someone whom we have loved, and when we ourselves approach the end of life, His authority over life and death becomes our source of strength and courage. Jesus wept at the grave of Lazarus because He felt the loss of a friend and because He shared the grief of the sisters. But His grief was not an impotent sentimentality. The authority of His lordship compelled the grave to give up its victim; Lazarus was restored to life. "I am He that liveth, and was dead; and behold, I am alive for evermore, Amen, and have the keys of Hades and of death" (Rev. 1:18). His people are in His keeping, and He is able to bring life out of death.

Responses of Obedience to the Lordship of Christ

How is the lordship of Christ made practical? There are four steps.

The first is to *learn His purpose*. This purpose may be disclosed by some new understanding based on God's Word. As the Holy Spirit applies it to our lives, it will bring a gradual but increasingly insistent conviction of what the next decision ought to be. Long-range purposes, like a call to service in some particular place, are entirely possible; but usually we see only the next step. Frequently, the door of opportunity opens when we bump our nose on it. An open mind and a prayerful spirit will bring consciousness of divine direction in life.

The second step is to *accept His purpose*. God does not hand the Christian a blueprint for his career. He proceeds by directing one step at a time. Obedience involves the acceptance of the purpose for the immediate future, trusting Him for the outcome of life as it unfolds.

When the next step becomes apparent, there must be a cheerful acceptance of it. Sometimes it presents difficulties to be surmounted. Sometimes its requirements may seem disagreeable or even irrational. Faith enters at this point. A step in the dark is not dangerous when suggested by a friend who knows the way. When God speaks, we must follow His command, or else the opportunity may be lost forever.

A young man who had dedicated his life to God for His service felt convinced that his place would be in Africa, and applied to a mission board for that field. The board informed him that there was a great need in Vietnam, and asked him to go there. Feeling that it was the call of God, he agreed, and was sent there. In the years of his ministry in that land, he and his wife opened a pioneer work among the aboriginal hill tribes that had been previously unreached, sponsored a new translation of the Bible into their language, and laid the foundation for a completely new life for a neglected people. Undoubtedly, their labors would have been fruitful in any place, but the direction of 50 years ago has been confirmed by the results apparent today.

The third step is to *obey promptly*. A soldier in the army does not tell the commanding officer that he will take the latest order under consideration. He must obey instantly, for the crucial turning point of a campaign may be involved. Likewise, God's commands to the members of His church must be obeyed at once, or disaster may follow. God's ultimate purpose may not be frustrated, but the privilege of participating in it may be denied to the disobedient. When King Saul failed to complete the assignment that God had entrusted to him, the Prophet Samuel said to him, "To obey is better than sacrifice, and to hearken than the fat of rams" (1 Sam. 15:22). Because of his disobedience, Saul forfeited the kingdom, and God's purpose was fulfilled by others.

The fourth step is to *prove the obedience*. In a parable quoted by Luke, Jesus contrasted two men who built their houses, one on sand, and the other on rock (Luke 6:47-49). When the floods came, the house on the sand was washed away because its foundation dissolved in the swirling waters. The house on the rock remained unmoved, because the ledge on which it was constructed was unyielding. The life which is disobedient to the lordship of Christ may seem prosperous while all circumstances are favorable. But when the situation changes, it collapses and is swept away. The life that is built on obedience to the known will of God abides forever.

On a hill overlooking the Connecticut River in Northfield, Massachusetts, is a stone marking the grave of D.L. Moody. He began his career as a shoe salesman, and was engaged in business when he was led to Christ by his Sunday School teacher. He had little education, and although successful in business, was apparently unfitted to become a public figure. Upon his conversion he began to engage immediately in evangelism, to the best of his ability. He was greatly impressed by a remark of Henry Varley, an English evangelist: "The world has yet to see what God can do with a man wholly dedicated to Him."

Moody replied, "By the grace of God, I will be that man." As he followed God's leading through his life, he brought revival on two continents, founded two schools, and left behind him a multitude of men and women who profoundly influenced their generation for God. On his gravestone are inscribed these words:

The world passeth away, and the lust thereof; but he that doeth the will of God abideth forever.

(1 John 2:17, ASV)

Moody had learned the secret of obedience to the lordship of Christ.

3
Can You Take It?

"Can ye drink of the cup that I drink of?"   Mark 10:38

A small procession was following Jesus as He slowly trudged up the rocky road from Galilee to Jerusalem. The way was long and steep, and at times the heat became oppressive.

Jesus' silence indicated that He was unusually serious. On at least two occasions, He had declared to them that He would die in Jerusalem (Mark 8:31; 9:31); and as they began this last stage of the journey from Jericho, He seemed to be increasingly preoccupied. The emotional conflicts within His own mind created a tense atmosphere in the group. Jesus had hoped that the disciples might understand the impending crisis, and longed for their sympathetic support.

The disciples, however, had a different concern. Throughout Jesus' ministry He had promised a kingdom in which they would be seated on twelve thrones judging the twelve tribes of Israel (Matt. 19:28). Since the disciples lived under the domination of the pagan Romans, they were enchanted by the prospect of becoming rulers of a kingdom. They hoped that Jesus was planning a coup to unseat the Jewish hierarchy that compromised with Rome, and to inaugurate the ideal state of freedom and prosperity.

Obviously they did not comprehend the situation from Jesus' viewpoint. They were thinking in terms of political liberty; He was contemplating a spiritual battle. They saw the program from the standpoint of national liberation; He was planning the redemption of a world. The scope of His outlook was wider than theirs, and involved a much longer and fuller campaign.

They *did* recognize that a crisis was imminent, and that if He and they were to emerge from it triumphantly, they should have a plan for action. If He intended to set up a new government, officers should be appointed. What better opportunity would there be for making sure of official positions as His assistants? Not only would such an arrangement be good policy, but it would ensure favorable privileges to those who acted first.

With this strategem in mind, James and John, the sons of Zebedee, approached Jesus with their request. Matthew, in a variant account (Matt. 20:20-27), tells how they enlisted their mother to present the request for them.

Since they must have been aware of the magnitude of their request, they approached Jesus obliquely by asking Him to grant whatever request they might make. He was too discerning to be caught by giving immediate assent, and replied, "What would ye that I should do for you?" They said, "Grant to us that we may sit, one on Thy right hand, and one on Thy left, in Thy glory." They wanted the two most prominent positions that a monarchy could offer—first assistants to the king.

The request was not inherently wrong and did not reflect disloyalty. John and James showed confidence in Christ's ulti-

mate triumph and a willingness to share in the coming conflict. But they had no real understanding of what that conflict
would be, nor did their attitude reflect Jesus' mood. He was
thinking of service, not of sovereignty; of sacrifice, not of success; and of submission, not of supremacy.

The fact that this was at least the third time Jesus had announced His coming death to the disciples showed how insensitive they were. They had grasped His idea of a kingdom, but
regarded it more as an opportunity for themselves than as a
fulfillment of divine purpose.

When Jesus began the last journey to Jerusalem by sending
messengers to ask for passage through a village of Samaria,
they were rudely rebuffed. James and John proposed that
they should call down fire from heaven to consume the inso-
lent Samaritans. Jesus rebuked them because their vehe-
mence reflected a total misunderstanding of His mission.
They had no concept of service by suffering (Luke 9:51-56).

Peter reacted in the same way when Jesus pointed out that
property was not an index of divine favor. Jesus had said that
it would be easier for a camel to pass through the eye of a
needle than for a rich man to enter the kingdom of God (Mark
10:25). Peter protested that he and the other disciples had left
their homes, their trade, and their possessions to follow Jesus,
and he asked what their recompense would be. It was plain
that Peter's chief concern was the advantage that would ac-
crue to him because he had become a follower of the Messiah,
rather than an overwhelming passion for the establishment of
the kind of kingdom that Jesus had in mind.

Redemption Is Paradoxical
The request of these disciples brought into sharp relief the
impending crisis. For Jesus it was the turning point of His
career. Either He must offer the sacrifice of His life for the
redemption of the world, or else adopt the disciples' philoso-

phy of putting personal interests first. His position is well
stated in the words at the conclusion of this episode: "For the
Son of man also came, not to be ministered unto but to minister, and to give His life a ransom for many" (Mark 10:45, ASV).
For the disciples, there was a choice—to follow Him completely in the way that God had planned, or else to desert
Him and revert to living for themselves only. Jesus discerned
both their good intentions and their inherent weakness, and
made them face the issue squarely by His penetrating challenge: "Can ye drink of the cup that I drink of; and be baptized with the baptism that I am baptized with?" (Mark 10:38)
In other words, "Can you take it?"

Jesus did not want to promise a privilege to James and John
without making plain to them that it would be accompanied
by responsibilities. If they should be allowed to sit with Him
on His triumphal throne, they must be ready to pay the price.
He did not refuse them the award, but insisted that they
should earn it. The words that He used metaphorically conveyed the prospect of struggle and of intense suffering. *Cup*
was an anticipatory reference to the prayer of Gethsemane, in
which He said, "Father, all things are possible unto Thee.
Take away this cup from Me; nevertheless, not what I will,
but what Thou wilt" (Mark 14:36).

For Him the cup meant misunderstanding. His enemies
had failed to comprehend His nature and His motives. If He
healed on the Sabbath, they saw Him only as the transgressor
of a commandment, and not as a saviour of humanity. He was
perpetually the victim of misinterpretation because He was
speaking to a generation lacking spiritual sense. The frustration of trying to penetrate the obtuseness of the minds of His
hearers was part of the *cup*.

The crowds viewed Him as a magician who performed
spectacular deeds, but were unwilling to accept Him as one
who could solve their problems. They marveled at the wis-

dom of His words, but refused to accept the truth contained in them. They were dazzled by the vehicle of His truth, and remained impervious to the truth itself. Could they, once they had understood the meaning of His mission, endure the same obstinate rejection that He had encountered?

The *cup* meant also for Him the injustice of a sentence demanded by malice and pronounced by expediency, the disgrace of a criminal's execution, desertion by His friends and the sting of betrayal by one of them, and the physical torture of crucifixion. Most difficult of all, it meant the clouding of the face of God and the apparent inconsistency of the fulfillment of the divine commission which ended in personal disaster. If these men were to have the triumph which He had promised, they must share His suffering. Would they be able to endure it?

The word *baptism* referred substantially to the same experience. Jesus remarked on one occasion, "I have a baptism to be baptized with, and how am I straitened till it be accomplished!" (Luke 12:50, ASV) Baptism was a figure of death. It symbolized laying down one's life to take it again by a new dynamic and for a new purpose. Jesus' mission was limited until He defeated death by submitting to it, and then by rising again as the unscathed and eternal Victor. For the disciples the parallel would be the surrender of their ambitions, desires, and prospects to apparent loss and futility, with the faith that the purpose of God would make that surrender the entrance into a larger and more effective life.

High Intention Is Vulnerable

The response of the disciples indicated that their loyalty was as great as their ignorance. At that point in their experience, they could not have comprehended all that Jesus' challenge involved. The answer that they gave to Him, "We are able," illustrated both their rashness and their resolution. It was rash because, in a moment of well-intentioned enthusiasm, they promised more than they could deliver. They had courage, but did not reckon with their own weakness. Peter was the classic example of this tendency. When Jesus told him that all the disciples had become the targets of Satan, and that he had been the object of special prayer, Peter confidently asserted that he was ready to go with Jesus to prison or death. Within a few hours, Peter blatantly denied that he ever knew Jesus (Luke 22: 54-62). In spite of this knowledge of their vulnerability to pressure, Jesus accepted their expressed intention as the true index of their spiritual purpose, and then held them to their word. He believed in their fundamental sincerity, despite the wretched failure that they made.

Jesus' initial response to their bold declaration of their ability to bear His burdens and to share His fate was positive. He assured them that they would indeed share His conflict and His triumph. It would be impossible to stay with Him without participating in the coming struggle.

Any follower of Christ must be prepared for misunderstandings, falsehoods, discriminations, deprivations, and even defeats and death. Immunity to these things cannot be guaranteed by any legislative machinery or by any cultural tradition. Even living in a pluralistic society, where freedom of religion is practiced, does not ensure freedom from attack; for the teaching of Jesus admits no rivals. If the disciples wished to be members of His kingdom, they had to be willing to pay the price of the membership.

Jesus took them at their word, and He promised them that they would indeed drink His cup and share His baptism. When He called them to follow Him, He knew well what that discipleship would entail. He knew also that considerable education would be necessary before they realized the meaning of discipleship. He would not release them from their commitment, even though they understood it only partially and fulfilled it only superficially. The deepening of character that they needed could be achieved only through participation in His experience.

Prayer for the realization of a full Christian experience is dangerous, not because God desires to imperil those who love Him, but because sharing in the triumph of Christ always involves the experience of the cross. The choice depends on a person's values: whether ease without Christ is worth more than suffering with Him, and whether the motive for endurance is a reward or devotion to His service. The early Moravian missionaries had as their slogan, "To win for the Lamb that was slain the reward of His sufferings;" and to that end they devoted their lives. The words echo the statement of Paul: "I have suffered the loss of all things . . . that I may know Him, and the power of His resurrection, and the fellowship of His sufferings . . . if by any means I might attain unto the resurrection of the dead" (Phil. 3:8-11).

Any man who enlists for service in the armed forces commits himself to hardship. He is abruptly severed from his family. He surrenders his individuality and becomes a cog in a military machine. He undergoes rigorous training: forced marches, carrying a heavy pack of equipment; slogging through rough fields and slimy swamps; exposure to extreme heat and cold; irregular and sometimes insufficient meals; simulated battle conditions under live fire; and exertion to the point of exhaustion. These conditions he accepts as incidental to his service, because he is preparing for the exigencies of warfare on which the fate of his nation may depend. He does not choose the hardships for their own sake; but he realizes that without the discipline that they demand, he will not be able to maintain his position. In similar fashion, the Christian's calling demands endurance to the end. Jesus never promised His followers more suffering than He had Himself. All that the world gave Him was a cross; how could they expect anything else?

As to the reward that the disciples requested, Jesus did not promise the highest seats to the ambitious pair, but neither did He absolutely deny them. Whether or not John and James would attain to the places they sought was left open, contingent upon the judgment of God. Jesus did not minimize the merit of loyalty, but He magnified instead the importance of humble service. He demonstrated this principle very effectively when, as their Master, He stooped to wash their feet when they would not undertake that menial task for each other. "Whosoever would be great among you, shall be your minister; and whosoever of you would be the chiefest, shall be servant of all" (Mark 10:43-44).

The proper motive is not self-exaltation, but service. James and John had taken the wrong road to the right goal. Endurance of humility is more productive of lasting effect than reckless pursuit of fame and fortune. To implement this motive calls for readiness to endure hardship, and persistence to the end in the face of opposition.

First Class Is Expensive

Life involves a choice that needs to be made intelligently, deliberately, and irrevocably. Before requesting special relationship with God, it is wise to count the cost.

If you must choose between a costly piece of goods and a cheaper one, you calculate whether you can pay the price for the one that is more valuable. The cheaper one may involve less strain on your pocketbook, but will it remain satisfactory over the years ahead? Is it better to pay more in order to have a more durable and efficient possession? The old dictum, "You get what you pay for," is valid in the spiritual life as well as in the marts of trade. A first-class experience with God has a high price on it, and it also brings lasting joy.

If we ask the best from Christ on His terms, we must accept

the responsibility that accompanies it. Great spiritual experiences are produced in the tension between the acceptance of a divine commission and the sense of personal inadequacy. Opposition, privation, fears, threats, and frustrations conspire to discourage and defeat us. As God slowly conducts us through our problems, we gain confidence in Him and learn to believe Him for greater achievements. Sometimes the acceptance of a task we do not understand becomes our compulsive motive to do it well and to triumph over handicaps.

An outstanding example of this principle is Joni, a girl who suffered complete paralysis of her body because of a broken neck. At first, existence seemed worthless, and she would have welcomed death rather than anticipate a lifetime of uselessness and dependence. She dared, however, to give her seemingly broken life entirely to Christ, trusting Him to use it in spite of her suffering. Today, as an accomplished artist, she paints by holding the brush in her teeth, and is able to exhibit victory over her pain and helplessness. The handicap itself has become an instrument for God. Both her artistry and her victorious spirit attest to the genuineness of her faith and the power of God in a life that seemingly had been ruined.

Suffering, furthermore, is often the best proof of the believer's faith. It throws into sharp relief the difference between the cynical complacency of wickedness and the uncompromising stand of righteousness. When a profession of faith demands great personal cost, that faith has to be much more than a mere veneer of religiosity or a hypocritical pretense. Jesus' challenge, "Are ye able?" was intended to make the disciples count the cost before demanding the privilege that they wanted.

To ask for prominence may not be wrong, but if the request is granted we must accept the price that goes with it. Yet the price itself is a reward, for the hardships are not an exile to solitary suffering, but an introduction to companionship with

Christ. We can understand Him only as we share His needs, His sorrows, His compassion for those who are downtrodden and forsaken, and the misunderstanding and rejection that He predicted. Perhaps Paul had this text in mind when he wrote to Timothy, "If we died with Him, we shall also live with Him; if we endure, we shall also reign with Him" (2 Tim. 2:11-12, ASV).

The Christian life is not an idyllic state of being "carried to the skies on flowery beds of ease." It is an endurance contest which requires the exertion of all one's strength and the perseverance of determination. To be sure, the strength and the persistence are supplied by God, who works in us "to will and to do of His good pleasure" (Phil. 2:13). The Christian life is not, however, a faith to coddle weaklings, but rather is a means of gaining new power.

Some years ago the Wheaton College faculty used to hold their fall retreat at the same camp where the football team drilled for the season. After the day's session ended, we would go to the practice ground to watch the players. Usually we arrived when the practice was ending, just before the evening meal. The boys were hot, tired, thirsty, and sore from the scrimmage of the afternoon. When the practice closed and they were blissfully anticipating showers, steaks, and sleep, the coach lined them up and made them run around the field three times at top speed. Stumbling and gasping for breath, with their tongues hanging out and with perspiration oozing from every pore, they doggedly circled the field three times, and then went off to the showers.

Why did the coach require that extra effort from them? He was not a sadist, but he knew that the winning team is not always the largest, the strongest, or the smartest. It is rather the team that stays on the field to the end, and that can endure when its opponents are ready to quit. The team that can "take it" is the team that gains the championship.

James and John wanted to be rated as champions, but Jesus wanted to know if they could "take it." Would they follow Him through the dangers of a trip to Jerusalem? Would they listen to His words when they did not understand what He was saying? Would they share with Him the loneliness and terror of Gethsemane? Would they remain loyal during the horror of the cross?

So He asked the question, "Are ye able?" He still asks it. We who now see the cross from the perspective of the past, and who recognize it not only as a potential threat but as an actual inevitability, must answer the same searching inquiry. A Christian is not an ambitious robot, devoid of any goal in life. He is not a log floating on the tide, passively waiting for something to happen. His calling is to serve the Lord Jesus Christ by fulfilling the objective of his redemption. Salvation implies that God has a definite purpose in saving man. This purpose can be achieved only by accepting Jesus' challenge to labor with Him and to endure, "as seeing Him who is invisible" (Heb. 11:27). Not with a boastful self-confidence, but with humility and faith, we should reply, "We are able."

> The Son of God goes forth to war
> A kingly crown to gain;
> His blood-red banner streams afar,
> Who follows in His train?
> Who best can drink His cup of woe
> Triumphant over pain,
> Who patient bears His cross below,
> He follows in His train.

4
Have You Done Your Homework?

"Have ye not read in the book of Moses how . . . God spoke unto him, saying, 'I am the God of Abraham, and the God of Isaac, and the God of Jacob'?"   Mark 12:26

The emergencies of life confront us at the most unexpected times. Whether they come in the form of situations in which we must act, of questions that we must answer, or of persons with whom we must deal, we need to be ready. Generally, there is little time for consideration of options or for deliberation on choices. The response is immediately necessary, and for better or for worse we must give it.

It is, of course, impossible to be prepared in detail for every contingency. Human experience is never wide enough to enable one to face every problem with assurance. On the other hand, it is possible by consistent discipline to be ready for

44

most of them. An airplane pilot cannot be prepared to react to every kind of storm that he may encounter. But he can be so well acquainted with operational procedures that he will be able to tell instantly by his instruments and by the "feel" of the plane how he should proceed.

In his Gospel, Mark narrated the story of a question that Jesus posed to a group of Sadducees. They were endeavoring to discredit Him by placing Him in a dilemma. They sketched a hypothetical situation in which a certain woman was married to the oldest of seven brothers. Before the couple had any children, the husband died. According to Jewish law, his next younger brother was required to take her as his wife in order that the deceased brother might have an heir to carry his name. The second brother died without issue, and the process was repeated to the third brother, and down to the seventh. All seven of them married her in succession, until finally she died also. "In the resurrection," the Sadducees asked, "whose wife shall she be?" (Mark 12:23)

Ridiculous as the question may seem to us, it had a deep meaning for the Sadducees. They used it to prove that there could be no resurrection. If there were a resurrection in which the conditions of this life were perpetuated, the law would contradict itself, for it would be promoting polyandry because she would belong to all seven brothers. By inference, they concluded that since the law could not teach anything inconsistent with itself, a resurrection would be impossible. It is true that the Old Testament has little to say concerning life after death. Clear statements do not appear frequently in the Torah (Pentateuch), and only occasionally in the Prophets. The Sadducees concluded that there could be no resurrection, and consequently denied the doctrine entirely.

This fanciful conundrum was intended to be the trap for Jesus. If He asserted boldly that any or all of the brothers would claim her for a wife, then He would be accused of questioning the ethical character of the law. If He agreed with them that there would be no resurrection, then He would be roundly condemned by the Pharisees, the more popular and influential theological party in Judaism.

Jesus did not accept either conclusion, but turned the whole dilemma back upon His antagonists with the disturbing enquiry, "Have ye not read? . . ." He challenged their scholarship by implying that they had not studied the evidence carefully. They had failed to read God's revelation with a discerning eye and to appreciate its spiritual implications. They were like students who asked foolish questions because they had not done their homework.

The Sufficiency of Revelation

Jesus' reply had certain important implications. First of all, He assumed the sufficiency and reliability of the revelation that they had. The law of Moses was the written Word of God accepted by all the Jewish people, including the Sadducees. They regarded the other books of the Old Testament as secondary authority, but adhered unswervingly to the authority of the Pentateuch. When Jesus quoted it to them, they could not consistently deny its authority. He pointed out that they had erred, not the law.

Since they had attempted to make a case by drawing an inference, He did the same; yet He began with a different type of text. They had taken an incidental law relating to the social practice of marriage; He referred back to a basic theological principle. The passage which He quoted (Ex. 3:6) is the self-declaration of God concerning His own nature and His relationship to the Jewish nation: "I am the God of thy father, the God of Abraham, the God of Isaac, and the God of Jacob."

In this utterance God asserted to Moses His eternal being and purpose. When God summoned Moses to become the deliverer of His people, Moses asked Him by what authority he should command Pharaoh to release the people from slavery. Unless Moses could demonstrate an authority greater than that of Pharaoh, he would have no prospect of success.

As the God of the three progenitors of the nation, Jehovah was the God who spanned the generations and whose purpose for the future was guaranteed. He was not a fictional deity devised by a religious adventurer and existing only in his imagination.

To Abraham He was the *God of promise* who planned the future. To Isaac He was the *God of power* who protected him from his enemies and preserved his line from extinction. To Jacob He was the *God of providence* who kept him through the years of his wanderings and finally reclaimed him by transforming him.

The concept of resurrection is an extension of the character of God who *promises eternal life* in Christ, *demonstrates His power* by the resurrection of Christ, and *effects final redemption* when He raises people from the dead.

This particular text, however, speaks more by inference than by declaration. Jesus drew the conclusion for the Sadducees by pointing out that God is not the "God of the dead, but of the living, for all live unto Him" (Luke 20:38). If, then, He is the God of the living, there must be more beyond human existence than extinction in physical death. Jesus was justified in drawing this inference because He was arguing from the nature of God, rather than from a social custom which was irrelevant to the original question.

The Progression of Revelation

The content of revelation is progressive. God did not disclose all truth at once. Revelation is something like a flower: First there is a seed, then there is a plant that bears a bud, then the bud expands into a flower, and finally the blossom becomes the full fruit. The concept of resurrection is germinal in the nature of God, the Source of life. He is a living God, the very opposite of death, by whom the process of life is originated, continued, and culminated according to His purpose.

In the Old Testament, there are allusions to the concept of personal survival beyond the grave. Jacob spoke of going down to Sheol to his son, when he learned of the presumed death of Joseph (Gen. 37:35). Sheol was the place of the dead where there was consciousness, but neither joy nor hope. The same concept appeared in the remark of David concerning the child of Bathsheba who had died: "I shall go to him, but he shall not return to me" (2 Sam. 12:23). Through the rest of the Old Testament are similar hints of belief in an afterlife. Job, despondent because of his physical distress and because of the apparent injustice of the calamities that had befallen him, cried out, "If a man die, shall he live again?" (Job 14:14), and later affirmed "I know that my Redeemer liveth, and that He shall stand at the latter day upon the earth; and though after my skin worms destroy this body, yet in my flesh shall I see God" (19:25-26).

Psalm 16, which Peter quoted on the Day of Pentecost, is more positive: "Thou wilt not leave my soul in Sheol, neither wilt Thou permit Thine Holy One to see corruption. Thou wilt show me the path of life. In Thy presence is fullness of joy; at Thy right hand there are pleasures for evermore" (Ps. 16:10-11).

The final answer to the question was provided through the climax of revelation, Jesus Himself, "who hath abolished death, and brought life and immortality to light through the Gospel" (2 Tim. 1:10).

The Responsibility of Revelation
Jesus' question implied that the Sadducees were not as informed about the subject of the resurrection as they should

have been. The Scriptures were in their possession, but they had not read them; or if they had read them, they did not do so with understanding. They were more interested in finding something over which to dispute than to discover God's will and obey it. They read the Scriptures with a veil over their minds and missed what was really important. If they were able to draw conclusions from what was irrelevant, they should have been as able to deal with what was relevant.

Jesus Himself lived by the Scriptures which He applied consistently to Himself. In them He found the program for His life marked out by the will of God. When He said, "How readest thou?" (Luke 10:26), He asked not simply for a quotation, but for an understanding of its sense.

God has revealed His nature, His attitude toward men, His commandments, and His purpose in the Scriptures. From the earliest chapters of Genesis to the final chapters of Revelation, there is one continuous disclosure of what we need to know in order to make contact with Him. Not all of the sections of the Bible deal with these truths in the same way nor suggest the same applications of them. Some of the teaching is pictorial, illustrated from the lives of God's servants. Some of it is historical, showing how God has operated in human experience through the discipline of His people and through the rise and fall of nations. Some is transmitted by command through His servants the prophets. Some truths were given by direct teaching of Jesus or through the apostles. All Scripture has been recorded under the control of the Holy Spirit and for our benefit, and we have a more extensive revelation than did the generation connected with its production. Our perspective on the law about which the Sadducees inquired is much broader than theirs, and should enable us to understand many things that were obscure to them.

For this reason our responsibility is greater. We have all kinds of aids to interpretation that modern discoveries have made available. No other book in history has undergone the detailed examination to which the Bible has been subjected. Whether it is devotedly studied by its friends to ascertain the promises and directions that God has provided for them, or whether it is dissected by its foes who wish to expose supposed discrepancies and thus to devaluate its authority, the Bible has received more attention than any other single piece of literature. It has been translated into more languages and has been quoted by more speakers and writers than any other known book.

Yet ignorance of the Bible is surprising. It has been neglected by the sophisticated, distorted by cultists, misrepresented by the ignorant, and discarded by skeptics. If Jesus was critical of the Sadducees because they had not examined the Scripture more closely when it existed only in scroll form, how much more would He be impatient with a more literate generation who never bother to read it in print?

Whenever one buys a new car, he is given an instruction manual which describes the features of his automobile, and tells how to operate and maintain it. If he is a wise man, he will read the manual carefully so that he may obtain the best possible service from his car. The manual will inform him how to avoid misuse of the mechanism, how to repair it, and how to operate it under differing weather and road conditions. If he fails to observe the manufacturer's directions, he cannot complain if at some time the automobile breaks down or suffers damage.

Our Creator has revealed to us in His written Word the secrets of spiritual adjustment: how we can relate to Him as the Source of our life, where to find supplies of strength and wisdom, how to avoid the pitfalls of temptation and carelessness, how to plan for a successful life, and how to set the goals that we should achieve. If we pay no attention to these, we have only ourselves to blame for our failures.

Methods of Studying Scripture

Everyone who aspires to knowledge needs to learn how to study. The process is not complicated, nor need it be burdensome. There is a thrill in the exploration of God's truth and in the daily discoveries that it produces. Jesus' answer to the Sadducees includes at least three suggestions for study.

1. Read in context. It is possible to isolate some one section or verse and to misapply it because the portion has not been interpreted in the light of the whole. The Sadducees summarized correctly the levirate law of marriage:

If brethren dwell together, and one of them die, and have no child, the wife of the dead shall not marry outside the family unto a stranger; her husband's brother shall go in unto her, and take her to him as his wife, and perform the duty of a husband's brother unto her. And it shall be, that the firstborn whom she beareth shall succeed in the name of his brother who is dead, that his name be not put out of Israel (Deut. 25:5-6).

This text was intended to deal with a sociological situation in order to avert the extinction of a family name. The plain sense they evidently understood. Their error lay in making it the foundation for a theological dogma.

There are, of course, many theological implications in Scripture which may legitimately be derived by inference from passages that are not primarily theological in character. These can be corroborated or corrected by reference to other sections of the Scriptures which relate directly to the same subject. In this instance the Sadducees failed, for Jesus said to them, "Do ye not therefore err, because ye know not the Scriptures?" (Mark 12:24) They had failed to balance their conclusion from one text by the more explicit impression to be drawn from another.

Such failure can lead to theology that is out of focus. Error sometimes lies not in crass falsehood, but in overemphasis of one truth, preached exclusive of other truths. For instance, it is true that Jesus was a human being, not an alien creature from space. He participated in all human activities, suffered human ills, and died a human death. To emphasize His humanity accords with the facts of revelation; but to do so exclusively overlooks the fact that the eternal Word became flesh, and that in the human Jesus, the Son of God has appeared on earth.

Such imbalance of truth can be avoided by the wide reading and comparison of Scripture with itself. By such practice the total teaching with its proper balance of component parts becomes plain. It is like seeing a country by flying over it and noting how the physical features of the land and the roadways and cities are related to each other. The total view of a country or continent prevents a narrow provincial outlook. The full acquaintance with the Bible does the same for one's understanding of doctrine.

2. Pursue exact study. What does the text really say? What precise ideas do the words express, and how do the sentences convey the attitude and mind of the author? Jesus asked the Sadducees if they had read the section of Exodus that dealt with Moses at the burning bush. To *read* means not only to see and recognize the words, but also to grasp their meanings.

The Bible lays great emphasis on meditation, or thinking carefully concerning what one has heard or seen. God's "blessed man" of Psalm 1 finds that "his delight is in the law of the Lord; and in His law doth he meditate day and night" (Ps. 1:2). Meditation is not cultivating vacancy of the mind, or trying to empty one's brain of thoughts. It is rather like examining an object by turning it over so that every side can be scrutinized, and by applying every available test to ascertain its composition.

The meaning of Scripture is not always apparent at the first reading. Arthur T. Pierson, a well-known American expositor of the early years of this century, once said, "When I had read this text for the one hundredth time, the following idea occurred to me." He had read it and thought about it sufficiently so that he did not speak from a superficial impression, but from a lengthy consideration of all the possible inferences that might be drawn from it. Research concerning the background of a text must be augmented by painstaking evaluation of what it actually says.

3. *Apply the Word.* A Christian's homework is not done until he has made application. This is done both by appropriating for himself the instruction or example of the Scripture, and by putting it into action. Jesus said, "If any man will do His will, he shall know of the doctrine, whether it be of God, or whether I speak of Myself" (John 7:17). Just as a student of science will read his laboratory manual, master the details of procedure, and then complete his knowledge by conducting the prescribed experiment, so a Christian learns the principles of spiritual life by reading the instructions, meditating on them, and practicing them. Many principles which seem abstruse and difficult to understand become quite clear when they are put into action.

In the early days of the Korean church, prospective members were required to memorize the Gospel of Matthew for admission. One old gentleman, whose memory had been affected by age, tried to learn it, but each time he came before the elders of the church, he failed to pass the test. They would not relax the requirement, and he went away discouraged. He was sure that he could never be accepted into the fellowship of God's people. One day, however, he appeared before the session and recited the Gospel flawlessly from beginning to end. When the elders expressed amazement over his feat and asked him how he did it, he replied that he had learned a paragraph or two at a time and then had practiced it on his neighbors. The constant application of the words of the text in governing his daily life had fixed them in his mind.

His procedure was simple but effective. When one acts on something that he has heard or seen, it becomes fixed not only by the repetition of the words, but also by force of habit. Practical use of what is learned intellectually is essential.

The Essential Dynamic of Scripture

One further consideration should be mentioned. Jesus said that error was caused not only by ignorance of the Scriptures, but also by unfamiliarity with the power of God. When He referred to Moses' experience in the desert, He indicated that Moses had both a *recollection* of what God had done in the past for Abraham, Isaac, and Jacob, and a *personal experience* of God in the bush that burned but was not consumed. God spoke to Moses' eyes and ears in such a way that he could not escape from the reality that confronted him.

It may not be that any of us will see a bush irradiated by a flame that does not consume it. But along with the study of the Scriptures, there must come the illumination of the Holy Spirit, who opens our minds to truth and enforces it by experience. Along with the Word of truth should come the realization that God is at work in our personal lives. As the application of Scripture brings the solution of problems that seemed insoluble, the conviction of truth becomes deeper, and error is less likely to occur.

The Sadducees were interested only in settling an argument; Jesus was presenting the key to a new life. The Sadducees had nothing to contribute to the hope and growth of those who listened to their dispute. Jesus could say, "The words that I speak unto you, they are spirit, and they are life" (John 6:63). It is the function of the Holy Spirit to interpret the words of Scripture to our minds, to apply them to our hearts, and to integrate them with our wills as we make each day's decisions.

The student who does not do his homework regularly may possibly pass the course by one last frantic effort; but he misses the value of the constant absorption of new knowledge which he can use as a growing resource of experience with which to meet emergencies. He will err in his judgments and constantly feel unprepared to meet the challenge of the day. In like manner, the Christian who does not do his homework will find that he easily becomes deluded, distracted, and defeated.

Ignorance of the Scriptures and of the power of God account for much weakness that exists in the modern church. The growth of the cults that advocate erratic or misleading doctrines would be greatly curbed if professing Christians knew what the Bible really teaches. A friend of mine, who served many years on the mission field, told how a modern cult had invaded a town where he occasionally preached. The national pastor there was an avid Bible student who had memorized a large part of the New Testament. Whenever a representative of that cult began to support his propaganda by biblical quotations, the pastor would quote the whole context and show how the cultist's argument was a misrepresentation. The result was that the cultist was quickly discredited and soon disappeared. Knowledge of the Word eclipsed the spurious teachings of the ignorant.

There is no excuse for ignorance. In Jesus' day only the wealthy could afford a scroll of the Old Testament. Usually scrolls were confined to the synagogues, for the work of copying the Pentateuch would require many weeks of time. Today Bibles are published in every major language, with translations into other languages appearing frequently. Many people are still illiterate, but even they can hear the Scriptures read if they are within the Christian church. The Sadducees did study the scrolls, but they neither understood them nor applied them. They were ignorant, spiritually and practically.

Direction for the future depends on preparation done in the present. The question that the Sadducees raised was for them an academic exercise, but it emphasized the whole question of the future life. On the implication of a text intrinsically unrelated to the topic of the resurrection, they negated the entire concept. Jesus, by referring to the nature of God, produced a positive assurance.

To the ever present question, "If a man die, shall he live again?" Jesus replied with the affirmation that a living God can impart eternal life to His worshipers. In His own revelation of God, Jesus said, "Because I live, ye shall live also" (John 14:19).

The only authentic guide for the mysteries of life and death is the revelation of God that culminates in the Person of Christ, interpreted by the Holy Spirit. Through that revelation we receive our direction.

"Thy Word is a lamp unto my feet, and a light unto my path" (Ps. 119:105). By diligent application of our minds to that eternal Word, we can traverse the paths of this world with confidence and enter the next world with hope.

Let us do our homework!

5
Why Are You Afraid ?

"Why are ye fearful, O ye of little faith?"   Matthew 8:26

From the first moment of life, when a person is thrust into a cold and blinding world from the comfort and security of his prenatal environment, to his last gasp of death, when he passes through the veil into the realms of the unknown, he is constantly confronted by situations that are unexpected and for which he is totally unprepared.

The sense of incompetence and the threat of failure evoke the emotion of fear. As an inducement to caution, fear can be salutary, for it often will prevent the carelessness that could bring disaster. It can also be paralyzing, if it prevents a person from taking any risks, or chains him to narrow routines that are proven to be safe. Fear can bring hesitation which may cause one to miss an opportunity. It may unnerve a person so that he is incapable of doing that for which he is eminently fitted, or it may reduce him to a cringing coward if it takes control of his mind and will, and so cripple him for life.

Of course, one may adopt an attitude of bold resolution and determine not to be overcome by fear. Yet if he does so, he may minimize the actual peril, and so expose himself to calamity, or he may become a braggart whose courage is founded on imagination rather than on reality. At times even the bravest person is confronted by some situation that seems uncontrollable, and which arouses fear that he cannot quell. To brush aside all consciousness of danger may be merely whistling in the dark. Danger must be recognized and met courageously. But to live in constant fear is unhealthy, and not a part of a normal Christian life. When Jesus saw His disciples frantic with terror, He challenged them with, "Why are ye fearful, O ye of little faith?"

Jesus had been engaged in a long ministry of teaching and healing in the vicinity of Capernaum. As the crowd increased, their demands upon His time and energy became so great that He needed relief. He decided to move to the east side of the Sea of Galilee, where He was not so well known and where the crowds would be smaller. With His disciples, He embarked in one of the fishing boats for the region of Gadara to find a place where they might rest in solitude.

The Sea of Galilee, because of its location, is subject to sudden violent windstorms. Its surface is about 600 feet below sea level in a bowl-shaped depression, and is surrounded by precipitous hills. When the sun sets in the afternoon, a wind rises over the Mediterranean Sea and blows inland, bringing cold air with it. Upon reaching the rim of the lake, this cold air drops on the water as the warm air rises, and the lake is often churned into foam. Such winds are a common occurrence, but on some occasions they lash the water into fury. This is what probably happened in the Gospel account.

The disciples had not rowed very far when a tremendous wind came down upon the lake, driving them out into the center. Their craft was an open boat without a covered deck.

When the violence of the waves began to fill the boat with water, they found it difficult to row or steer and knew they were in danger of being completely swamped. The storm must have been exceptionally violent, for the disciples were hardened fishermen, accustomed to all the moods of the lake. Possibly they had undertaken this trip at Jesus' request, even though they thought it might be risky because of threatening weather. They were frantic with fear, for they realized that the boat was in imminent danger of sinking in the middle of the lake.

Jesus, however, was apparently unconscious of their peril, or else was not concerned for them. Exhausted by His labors of the previous days, He had fallen asleep on a cushion at the stern, and had not been awakened by the splashing of the water or by the pitching of the boat. Mark's account reports that the disciples reproached Jesus: "Master, carest Thou not that we perish?" (Mark 4:38) They felt that He should contribute to their effort to reach safety on the shore.

Jesus was not troubled by the storm. His faith in the Father's care was so strong that He could rest peacefully in the howling wind which tossed the boat like driftwood on waves threatening to engulf it. To the disciples He was a perfect example of calm trust in the sovereign God who is able to make all circumstances serve His purpose.

Causes for Fear

Fear was a very natural reaction to the disciples' situation. Against the powers of nature, the naked strength of man avails nothing. Their awesome forces make one feel helpless. Lightning can split a giant tree into toothpicks. A wind of hurricane force can level a forest. In a typhoon in Hong Kong, I have seen the wind folding massive I-beams as if they were constructed of cardboard. A flood will sweep roadways and houses before it, and will cut a channel faster than a fleet of bulldozers could do it. The Galilean disciples knew that their frail skiff could easily be wrecked on the shore or go down in the center of the lake. They were so overwhelmed by the storm that they forgot the power that Jesus had exercised in time past, and gave way to panic.

Why did Jesus rebuke them for a perfectly natural reaction? For one thing, they should have remembered that the God whom they served is the Creator and Lord of the forces that menaced them. If He made the winds and the water, He could control them. While He does not capriciously violate His own laws, He can make the forces of nature fulfill His purpose. If He could open the sea to let the people of Israel escape from Egypt, and if He could eliminate an invading army by a pestilence, He should be able to save thirteen people in one small boat. The disciples had forgotten their own national history. For them their immediate circumstances had eclipsed their memory of past deliverances.

Again, they had lost sight of the purpose of Jesus' ministry. He had come into the world to reveal the person and power of God. Repeatedly, He asserted that He had been sent by the Father. Certainly God did not intend that He should perish accidentally in a storm without discharging His commission. If that commission included the development of the disciples, no storm of wind could thwart God's intention of having Jesus fulfill His obligation and of preparing them to be His agents and successors.

Jesus did not stand aloof from danger, but shared the disciples' perils. They, on the other hand, were protected by His presence and power. However, they were not aware of this, for they did not yet realize His importance, and held too narrow a view of His powers and of His willingness to act on their behalf.

Finally, they were preoccupied with themselves and their danger, and temporarily lost the awareness of His presence.

Because He was not talking to them or performing some deed on which they could focus their attention, they lost their consciousness of Him. Like children who are fearful when their parents are out of sight, these men who were normally cool and self-reliant were emotionally disturbed because they had lost touch with their Protector. Jesus had given them ample proofs of His power to conduct them safely through danger, and they had not profited by the example.

Destructive Fear?

The words of Jesus indicate that fear is the opposite of faith. Fear is not an unbelief that denies some truth directly, but one which neglects to appropriate truth that is available. The disciples failed to appreciate the latent power in Jesus' presence, and became frightened because they measured their situation by the storm and not by Him. Their appeal to Him was prompted more by desperation than by confidence.

Fear is *disorganizing*. They were so overcome by terror that they could not work together efficiently. They were so uncertain of their safety that they could not organize themselves. Fear prevents the concentration of thought that can produce a remedy for the impending danger—if, indeed, there is any remedy.

Fear is *unreasoning*. It evokes an instinctive response of flight, or possibly of fury, if resistance is unavoidable. Under stress the resistance is usually more frantic than intelligent, and lacks the skill that is inspired by cool courage.

The occasion for fear may be physical danger. A fire, an automobile accident, a hurricane, or a sudden attack can unnerve one. Or it may be fear of failure—a scholar dreading the examination that he is about to take, or a businessman worrying lest his prospective deal will not be successful. It may be dread of a person who is hostile and with whose influence or malicious power one cannot cope. It may be the foreboding of a disease that gradually consumes bodily strength. It may be the shrinking from death or old age, with the accompanying loss of all that one has enjoyed and loved, and the uncertainty of an unknown future. Yet on each of these occasions, a Christian believer can hear the voice of Jesus; "Why are ye fearful, O ye of little faith?"

The Antidotes to Fear

One antidote to fear is *faith*. Jesus' searching question recalled the disciples to a positive confidence in Himself. The faith in God which He exhibited by sleeping peacefully though the windstorm revealed His perfect confidence in the power and purpose of His Father. As the representative of the Father, He presented Himself as the object of the disciples' faith and hope at that particular moment. Rising to His feet, He commanded the storm to be stilled, and it hushed like a child rebuked by its parent. To the amazement of the disciples, the lake suddenly became calm. And they said to each other, "What manner of man is this, that even the winds and the sea obey Him?" (Matt. 8:27)

How is this kind of faith developed? Faith is not a complacent feeling that somehow everything will turn out well. Sometimes everything does not and one may be severely disillusioned. Griefs, disappointments, and failures are the common lot of all humanity. The victory of faith does not consist in dodging the storms, but in finding the master of them.

The disciples had to realize first of all what the real power of Jesus was. According to the record of the synoptic Gospels, the event came rather early in Jesus' career, before the disciples had witnessed many of His miracles. They had, however, seen Him heal the sick, and they must have recognized that He possessed unusual powers. They did not apply what they already knew by trusting Him to do more than they had already witnessed. They should not have limited Him by thinking that He would be unable to deal with the powers of nature. *The first step of faith is to accept the power of Christ as a fact, and to call upon Him for that which is greater than what we have already experienced.*

Faith is *confidence*, not in circumstances, but in a Person. The disciples' appeal to Jesus showed that they expected Him to take part with them in the struggle to reach the land. Probably, they did not expect Him to quell the storm directly, as He did; but they did look to Him to lend His additional strength to their exertions. They assumed that He had their welfare at heart; and though their question was negative, they were counting on His permanent concern for them.

We who now live on the other side of that storm can understand that He was both able and willing to rescue them, and that He responded instantly to their appeal. The centuries have not changed Him, and the risen Christ is still aware of our dangers. He is ready to save us from the temptations and threats that confront us. He is still with us in our perils and calamities, to avert the damage that may befall us and the despair that may overwhelm us. "I am with you always," He said, "even unto the end of the age" (Matt. 28:20).

Faith is *acceptance* of the purpose of God. Jesus Himself was aware of the storm of opposition through which He must pass and of the tragic outcome at the cross. For Him, the storm on the lake was only a passing incident in comparison with the trial that awaited Him. He never swerved from the path marked out for Him, because He knew that God had a purpose for Him that was greater than the perils encountered in achieving it. Because He was supremely confident in God's plan for His life, He did not seek to avoid them. Since He realized that His suffering would accomplish God's purpose, His love for the Father and His expectation of victory were sufficient to sustain Him in the darkest hour of His life.

As the purpose of God unfolds in our lives, we gain a constantly enlarging understanding of His objective, and we can acquire a growing faith in His ability to perfect that purpose. That confidence is an effective antidote to fear. Investing a life for God means that its outcome is securely guaranteed, even though the cost of the investment may be high. God never fails to attain His objective. For Jesus, it was attained at the price of the cross, which He faced without fear. For us who follow Him, there is no need for fear when we accept His purpose as He applies it to us.

Another antidote to fear is *love*. In conducting a wedding ceremony, I listen to the bride and groom pledge their vows to each other. In every instance when a bride is asked, "Wilt thou have this man to be thy wedded husband, to live together after God's holy ordinance of matrimony? Wilt thou love him, honor him, obey him, and keep him in sickness and in health, and forsaking all others keep thee only to him as long as you both shall live?" she answers firmly, "I will." She realizes that she is pledging herself unconditionally to a man whom she does not know perfectly and to a future that is as yet unrevealed. The bridegroom might prove to be a wastrel; misfortune could dog his steps; the marriage might be filled with sorrow and hardships, and end in tragedy. The future is unpredictable, and yet each bride commits herself fearlessly because she loves her bridegroom and believes that the best years lie ahead.

If in the variable chances of human life one person can so trust another without hesitation, how much more can we discard our fears when we put our trust in an omnipotent God whose love is unswerving and whose purpose is unchangeable? As one of Jesus' disciples wrote, "Perfect love casteth out fear" (1 John 4:18).

What is the result of faith? Jesus, the disciples, and the boat reached their destination safely. They met a new test there, but Jesus dealt with that successfully also. Stage by stage, come good or ill, He leads us forward in His triumphant procession. He does not evade the perils; rather He conducts us through them. Therefore let us discard our fears, and, assured that He is with us in our little boat, trust Him to calm the storm and bring us to our heaven. As Martin Luther wrote:

> And though this world with devils filled
>   Should threaten to undo us;
> We will not fear, for God has willed
>   His truth to triumph through us. . . .
>   Let goods and kindred go;
>   This mortal life also;
>   The body they may kill,
>   His truth abideth still.
> His kingdom is forever.

6
What's the Big Attraction?

"What went ye out into the wilderness to behold? A reed shaken with the wind? But what went ye out to see? A man clothed in soft raiment? . . . But wherefore went ye out? To see a prophet? Yea, I say unto you, and much more than a prophet." Matthew 11:7-9, ASV

Among the characters described in the New Testament, John the Baptist was one of the most colorful and significant. Born to his parents in their old age, he was chosen for a peculiar ministry which was about as unpopular as a prophet could pursue. He called for individual repentance, in a nation whose religious life was founded on community solidarity. He demanded confession of sin by baptism, from those who prided themselves on being the descendants of God's friend, Abraham (John 8:33).

In his denunciation of popular sins, John was blunt and uncompromising; and his directness of language alienated many. He actually seemed to delight in berating the respectably religious Pharisees, for he said, "O generation of vipers, who hath warned you to flee from the wrath to come?" (Matt. 3:7) Instead of capitalizing on his sensational approach to advertise himself, he insisted that he was not the person who should become the focus of attention. Rather, he pointed to another who would follow him with a larger and more important ministry.

Notwithstanding the fact that he broke almost every Madison Avenue rule for successful advertising, he gained a tremendous following. From all the cities and towns of the surrounding regions, the crowds poured out into the inhospitable wilderness to hear him. There were no lunchrooms, motels, or auditoriums where he preached; the ordinary amenities of his own culture were missing. And yet, his ministry was the sensation of the day, until he happened to incur the enmity of Herod.

Herod Antipas, the son of Herod the Great, was a playboy and a capricious tyrant. Although he professedly was a Jew, he had flouted both the spirit and the letter of the law when he stole his brother's wife, who was also his niece, and married her. His subjects were incensed by this flagrant violation of their sacred law, but could do nothing about it.

When John was preaching in the wilderness of Judea, Herod visited his meetings out of curiosity. Perhaps he suspected that John had political designs. Instead of recognizing Herod's royal presence by a few well-chosen words of welcome, John pointed his bony finger in the face of the adulterous king and rebuked him publicly: "It is not lawful for thee to have thy brother's wife" (Mark 6:18). Herod's wife was enraged, and Herod imprisoned John and later executed him.

While John was imprisoned, he sent a delegation of his

disciples to inquire of Jesus whether He were really the Messiah he had announced or whether another might be expected. Jesus answered them that His works would speak for Him.

As the emissaries turned back to tell John what they had seen, and heard, Jesus asked His audience what had made John so popular. Why had this lean, sunburned denizen of the desert been so attractive to the crowds that went to hear him preach? Why had his rough and blunt style appealed to them? Why should they have desired to listen to a message that demanded repentance, jarred their complacency, challenged their assumptions, and called for a radical personal commitment? At times John's language bordered on the abusive. His methods were unconventional and his predictions were seemingly improbable. After all, there had been many agitators and would-be messiahs in Judaism. Was this man simply another of them?

Jesus' Estimation of John

Jesus raised His questions in order to evaluate John in comparison with others of his kind. John had preached the kingdom of God (Matt. 3:2; Luke 3:1-17), and Jesus had followed with the same message (Luke 4:43). Jesus declared His appreciation of John's ministry for three reasons:

1. *A standard of truth.* "What went ye out . . . to see? A reed shaken with the wind?" In Galilee, along the edges of the Lake of Gennesaret and in the valley of the Jordan were many places where the long swordlike reeds grew luxuriantly. When the wind blew from the west, they bowed to the east; if the wind blew from the east, they leaned to the west. Since the reeds possessed no rigidity to stand against it, they swayed with the passing breezes. Jesus was pointing out that John did not attract his audience by compliance with the fashionable thinking of the day. He had a standard of truth

and adhered to it unfalteringly. The Law of God was his rule, and he could not make any exceptions to its requirements for Herod or for anyone else. His resolution matched his convictions, even when his loyalty to them cost him his life.

This quality of stern and unswerving adherence to the righteous Law of God aroused the admiration of the crowd. To be sure, there were probably few among them who would have had the courage to adopt John's stand and to declare it boldly as he did, or to live by it. Nevertheless, they honored him for it. Had he been willing to compromise, the crowd would have branded him as just one more demagogue seeking popularity at any price, and would have paid little attention to him. The man of principle is not always popular, but he is respected even by his enemies.

During the 1920s, when ecclesiastical tensions were running high and theological debate was heated, Dr. J. Gresham Machen became prominent in the controversy. He had challenged the appointment of some missionaries by the mission board of his denomination, because they would not subscribe to the statements of its official confession. He objected particularly to the theological position of Pearl Buck, who later left the mission field and became a well-known author. Their disagreement was irreconcilable, and the controversy was sharp. When Dr. Machen died in 1937 at the height of the debate, Pearl Buck paid him tribute, saying he had been a just and honorable opponent. She acknowledged that although he had condemned her divergence from the standard that she had agreed to uphold, he had never stooped to unjust or devious methods, or to personal vilification.

Compliance rather than conviction seems to be the mood of our decade. Anything is acceptable if a majority will vote for it. There is no recognition of authority other than the consensus of the moment. There may be protests of one kind or another; in fact, they have become fashionable, but they are based merely on the desires or feelings of a minority. Where is the man who will say, "Thus saith the Lord," and stick to that?

Back in the American colonial period, my ancestors, under the leadership of the Rev. Ezekiel Rogers, migrated from the small village of Rowley in northern England. Ezekiel Rogers was a stalwart Puritan. When he heard that King Charles I had issued a decree that there should be bowling on the village green on the Sabbath, he rebelled. Rather than comply with the royal order to announce the decree from his pulpit, he took almost his entire parish to America, where they founded another town by the same name. There they could live according to what they believed to be the Law of God. Ezekiel Rogers regarded the cost and effort of migration a fair price for freedom of conscience. He was not a "reed shaken with the wind."

This is the kind of conviction that Christians need. The ethical assumptions of popular trends creep subtly into the consciousness of Christians and gradually render them insensitive to the holiness that God expects of His people. While at times it may be necessary to make an organized protest against some rampant evil, the common resistance of personal conscience and conduct is far stronger. Righteousness as the lifestyle of Christians is more convincing than a new organization which appears merely to be bidding for financial support. The need today is not for more reforming societies, but for a public conscience.

2. *An inner integrity.* "But what went ye out to see? A man clothed in soft raiment? Behold, they that wear soft clothing are in kings' houses." People who are accustomed to the use of many kinds of fabrics may find this statement rather puzzling. Silks, cottons, and polyesters of various kinds for wear by common people were unknown in Jesus' day.

In the story of the rich man and Lazarus, Jesus described

the former as one who was "clothed in purple and fine linen" (Luke 16:19). Such clothing was restricted to the wealthy, for purple dye could be worn only by the upper classes, and fine linen was costly to manufacture. Even the sight of people who wore such goods was rare, and they would be regarded as a curiosity. Ordinary persons wore rough wool, often woven at home, or sackcloth made of goat's or camel's hair.

The implication of Jesus' words is that John was not a fashion plate whose elegant costume would excite the wonder of the masses. Nor was he a member of the upper class whose presence and utterance might be considered impressive. According to Matthew's account, John wore a loincloth of leather and a cloak or tunic of camel's hair—both products of the desert. His garments proclaimed his unpretentious status, and differentiated him from those who belonged to the "establishment," or who sought to gain office. If there was anything about him that attracted the crowd, it was certainly not any wealth or luxury that he flaunted.

To a certain degree, there is truth in the proverb that "clothes make the man;" however, one cannot be judged wholly by externals. Appearance is not the final criterion of importance. Neatness and cleanliness are commendable, but the inner life is really the true measure of the person. Jesus commended John the Baptist for the character he possessed, and not for his wardrobe.

David's prayer, "Behold, Thou desirest truth in the inward parts, and in the hidden part Thou shalt make me know wisdom. Purge me with hyssop, and I shall be clean; wash me, and I shall be whiter than snow" (Ps. 51:6-7), enunciates this truth. As king of Israel, David could wear the most elegant robes of his time but in dealing with God, he realized that only the inner life counted.

The power of John's ministry lay in his person and message, not in his external equipment. While it is true that modern facilities such as electronic communications, new methods of advertising, and other devices are valuable aids, the real secret of spiritual success is within the messenger himself. He is effective only to the degree that his message is derived from God and that his life is consistent with it.

3. *A prophetic message.* "But what went ye out to see? A prophet? Yea, I say unto you, and much more than a prophet." The prophets were God's spokesmen who applied the law to the life of Israel. They anointed kings, advised them in the affairs of state, rebuked the injustices of their society, encouraged the people in the times of depression, established schools of younger prophets, and often directed the kings in their foreign policies. The priests confined their activities largely to the ritual and to observance of religious duties. The prophets were independent preachers and statesmen who were inspired directly to declare "the Word of the Lord." Samuel was the chief mentor of the early years of the divided kingdom; Nathan was David's counselor during his long reign; Isaiah's ministry covered a lifetime in which he spanned the reigns of four monarchs; Uzziah, Jotham, Ahaz, and Hezekiah. Jeremiah was the prophet of the Exile, and Daniel became the representative of his people in Babylon.

From the time of Malachi, the voice of prophecy was strangely silent. Jesus said that "the Law and the Prophets were until John; since that time the kingdom of God is preached" (Luke 16:16). For this reason He said that John was more than a prophet, for he closed the line of those who were preparing for the advent of the kingdom of God, and became the herald of a new day. His predecessors had spoken of a coming Redeemer, but their knowledge was limited and their predictions fragmentary. They were chiefly concerned with the prevailing spiritual and political conditions of their time, and their projections of a future revelation were framed in the discussion of current needs.

John was more than a prophet because he was the immediate forerunner of the Messiah, sent as the messenger to prepare His way (Matt. 3:3; Mal. 3:1; Isa. 40:3). John's status was determined more by his message than by his office. He was recognized by the people as a prophet (Matt. 14:5), and for that reason they listened to him eagerly. Whereas the prophets as a class had spoken of the future kingdom that God had promised to the nation, John had a message of greater importance: that the kingdom had actually drawn near.

The Message of John

The preaching of John contained three new elements: the positive preparation for a definite person whose arrival was imminent; the identification of that person as the Lamb of God, the final sacrifice to take away sin; and the identification of the Son of God, the authentic representative of God in the flesh (John 1:23, 29, 34). In John the apex of prophetic preaching was reached. The great attraction was really the presentation of Jesus. "To Him give all the prophets witness, that through His name whosoever believeth in Him shall receive remission of sins" (Acts 10:43).

1. *Kingdom.* The imminence of the kingdom was the first topic of concern. If the Messiah were to accomplish anything, He must have a group of followers to whom He could reveal His plans and who would understand His purpose. The forerunner was obliged to provide them. John's ministry was intended to call out from the body of the Jewish people a group who would be individually desirous of finding the true Messiah, and who would be ready to accept His teaching when He came.

For this reason John stressed the importance of personal righteousness to be obtained by repentance. Then, after plainly stating that he was not the Messiah, he pointed to Jesus as the One on whom they should fix their attention. On this all the Gospels agree (Matt. 3:11-12; Mark 1:7; Luke 3:6-17; John 1:26-27). John proclaimed a new era, and was concerned much more with the person who was following him than he was with religious or political changes that might be effected by initiating an organization. He was so devoted to this Person that he later said of Jesus, "He must increase but I must decrease" (John 3:30).

In this respect the Christian witness is patterned after that of John. Paul said, "We preach not ourselves, but Christ Jesus the Lord, and ourselves your servants for Jesus' sake" (2 Cor. 4:5). There is always a tendency to enlarge upon our spiritual experience, our status and privileges, or upon our accomplishments. Certainly these may be the consequences and proofs of the reality of what Christ can do for each of us, but the focus of importance should be on the cause; the effects are secondary. Our Christian witness does not consist of a sanctimonious monologue about our spiritual character or achievements, but is rather a glorification of Christ. The song of heaven is not, "*I* arrived here," but "*Thou art* worthy" (Rev. 5:9).

2. *Sacrifice.* The second aspect of John's superprophetic declaration is a persistent emphasis on sacrifice. It began in Eden, where God countered the sin of man and its consequences by clothing him with the skins of slaughtered animals (Gen. 3:21). The first man clothed himself with an expedient of figleaves; God clothed him by an expiatory death. The first acts of worship were the sacrifices of Cain and Abel. Again, the sacrifice of the fruits of a cursed earth was rejected; the sacrifice of life was accepted. At the time of the Exodus, when God rescued His people from Egypt, the blood of a lamb on the lintel and doorposts of each house was their insurance against the judgment of death that was visited upon all the firstborn of Egypt. The law prescribed sacrifices and offerings for sin, which were immolated constantly in the temple wor-

ship while the Israelites were faithful to God. These sacrifices, although they were a recognition of the heinousness of sin and of its inevitable penalty, were not sufficient to meet the demand of God's Law. The sacrifice of an animal was emblematic of the death due to the sinner, but the animal could not adequately take his place.

The final sacrifice is the Lamb of God who came "to give His life a ransom for many" (Mark 10:45). "For if the blood of bulls and goats, and the ashes of an heifer sprinkling the unclean, sanctifieth to the purifying of the flesh, how much more shall the blood of Christ, who through the eternal Spirit offered Himself without spot to God, purge your conscience from dead works to serve the living God?" (Heb. 9:13-14) John announced Jesus as "the Lamb of God, who taketh away the sin of the world" (John 1:29). The promise of forgiveness through redemption is central to the message of the one who was "more than a prophet."

Redemption by a person rather than by an animal personalizes the entire concept. The animals were of no great intrinsic significance. They were sacrificed by the thousands, and not one of them would merit the gratitude and devotion of a man. John presented One who gave Himself for our sins. Through Him we are believers in God, for the death of Christ is the proof of God's love for us, and becomes the incentive to holiness, for He died that we might live for righteousness (1 Peter 1:18-22; 2:24).

3. *Authority*. The third aspect is even more astonishing: Jesus is the Son of God. The emphasis on the word *Son* is not so much to establish His origin as to describe His nature. When He said, "I came forth from the Father" (John 16:28), He thereby claimed a unique origin. But He usually mentioned His relationship to the Father as His source of authority. The Father had sent Him into the world as His personal representative, qualified to demand obedience. His revela-

tion of God would be authentic because of His filial connection, and the revelation that He transmitted to men through His person and words would be final. John was the forerunner, commissioned to proclaim His advent and to connect His revelation with that of the older dispensation.

John's special privilege was to announce the arrival of the full revelation of God in Christ. The previous prophetic messengers had exposed the sins of the people, but had not explained completely the purpose of God in salvation. The hints of it in their messages were like the sight of mountain peaks through a fog that yields occasional glimpses of the surrounding landscape, but does not provide a complete view of it. John was given a clear declaration of a person who had already appeared and whose message would be available. Redemption would no longer be a promised blessing, but an accomplished fact accessible to faith. The revelation of God would not be dependent on the symbolism of a ritual, but would be exemplified in a living person with whom they could enjoy close contact. With a message so defined and so demonstrated, there would be no excuse for unbelief.

Jesus reproached His generation for their unwillingness to hear John. He said that they were like children playing in the town square. If they imitated the musical festivities of a wedding, the others did not dance; if they wailed like mourners at a funeral, the others paid no attention to them. John came with his stern message of abstinence, and the people pronounced him a demoniac. Jesus tried to reach them by attending their feasts, and they accused Him of gluttony and drunkenness (Matt. 11:16-19).

By His questions, Jesus indicated that neither popular opinion, elite pronouncements, nor religious status is sufficient for establishing spiritual leadership. One must be "more than a prophet," and Christ is the only one who has a right to claim final authority. He came at the fullness of time

(Gal. 4:4), when the prophecies of the past had their fulfilment in His person, and when His advent made the forerunner more than a prophet. Christ brought reality to a symbolized redemption, and has made the final sacrifice to end all sacrifices.

In His person God has been adequately revealed in the arena of ordinary human life, not by a transcendent vision described in unfamiliar language, but by One who lived with fishermen, asked water from a woman of a despised alien race, wept at the grave of a friend, and died in physical agony. In experiencing all these things, He transcended them all; and returned triumphant from death.

The centurion at the cross echoed the declaration of John the Baptist; "Truly, this was the Son of God" (Matt. 27:54). To proclaim this message of Jesus as "the great attraction" can make Christian evangelism greater than the preaching of John the Baptist. As Jesus said, "I, if I be lifted up from earth, will draw all men unto Me" (John 12:32).

7
What's the Best Deal ?

"For what is a man profited, if he shall gain the whole world, and lose his own soul?"   Matthew 16:26

Many of us can remember the first car that we bought. It was probably the largest expense that we had undertaken up to that point, and we were quite uncertain how much we should spend. If we bought a cheap secondhand car, it might cost us much more in repairs than we paid for it originally. If we took out a loan to buy a shiny new one, the financial burden might be more than we could carry. The critical question was one of value. How could we obtain the best service for our needs at the least expense?

Later, other questions of value arose. Perhaps we married and needed a home. We asked ourselves, "Shall we buy an old house that is substantially constructed, but needing repairs that will take costly materials and time that could better be spent on other things? Or should we assume a 30-year mortgage that will really triple the sale price?" Such decisions were difficult, and whichever alternative was accepted, the house did not come cheap.

What Is Your Prime Asset?

Jesus posed a question to His disciples that involved a more drastic decision, for it affected not only their possessions, but also their persons. The chief issue was not money, but life. "For what is a man profited, if he shall gain the whole world, and lose his own soul?" He was not talking about risking a bank account on some investment that might or might not be profitable, but of expending one's whole personality to the best advantage.

Irrespective of how much or how little property you possess, there is one piece of capital that you have—your personality. Throughout life you are slowly expending it for the things that you consider to be most valuable. You are continually investing it, whether you realize it or not.

The word Jesus used to describe *personality* in this passage (Matt. 16:26; Mark 8:36; Luke 9:25) is *psyche*, from which *psychology* is derived. The word is commonly translated "soul," but its meaning has many aspects. It can refer to the nonphysical aspect of man in contrast to the visible and tangible body (Matt. 10:28). It can refer to the totality of life and experience that distinguishes the individual. Or it may be the inner conscious self that has its distinct identity and that persists through the varying stages of growth from birth to death, and presumably beyond death. Perhaps the best single word that will render it in modern speech is *personality*.

Throughout the course of life, each person is investing his personality in the things that seem to have the greatest value. Investment, however, can be a risky business. Financially, a man may buy a business that appears to be profitable, only to find that however sound the balance sheet may be, it is based on a vanishing market. No one today would buy a buggy-whip factory. Someone might buy at a bargain price a piece of real estate, only to discover that it was located in a deteriorating neighborhood where rising taxes and poor surroundings would soon erase the anticipated margin of profit. In the realm of material gain and loss, one must always exercise foresight and caution. The risk ought not to be so great that loss is almost certain. On the other hand, a good opportunity should not be overlooked.

What Are the Anticipated Profits?

When Jesus spoke of profit and loss, He was talking in terms of eternal values. Man was not created for time alone, but for eternity, and his values ought to be calculated accordingly. In the words of this text, Jesus declared the principle by which His disciples should gauge their decisions. What did He mean?

The text cannot be properly understood apart from the context in which it is set. Jesus had taken the disciples to the town of Caesarea Philippi, which was located far to the north of Palestine near the springs of the Jordan. It was a Gentile city in the territory of Philip, the son of Herod the Great. Philip had renamed it Caesarea in honor of Augustus Caesar, and had appended his own name to distinguish it from numerous other Caesareas in the Roman world. Probably in order to escape harassment by His opponents in Galilee, Jesus withdrew to Caesarea Philippi to confer privately with His disciples. His situation had become critical, and He needed to give them further instruction and to elicit from them a committal of loyalty. The impending event of the Cross made it necessary for them to declare their values. Would they, in the stress of the days before them, choose the safety and comfort of living for themselves? Or would they accept His values and adhere to Him at all costs? What was the best deal for their advantage?

Of the two alternatives, Jesus said more about the negative one. He regarded it as a bad risk, for to gain the whole world could easily mean losing one's own soul. Why is this true? Would not success in business or in one's own profession or trade bring a sense of self-assurance, the pleasure of having overcome obstacles, the attainment of leisure for personal comfort, and the certainty of adequate financial resources for enlarging and improving one's personality? Are grinding poverty and cultural deprivation necessary for personal development? Why do men choose the negative alternate?

1. *Prestige.* The inducements for gaining the world are alluring. Many men struggle for prestige because they wish to be regarded as important. Nobody wants to be a human cipher. In whatever circles one moves, he wants to be regarded as the boldest, or the most ingenious, or the most influential, or the wisest of that class. For such a reputation, he invests his whole personality, in order to attain fame.

Jesus never said that His disciples should be content with mediocrity. The very fact that they have been redeemed by the blood of Christ from sin and consequent disaster ought to be sufficient incentive to strive for excellence. If excellence is achieved, the prestige will often take care of itself; but it is not the main objective of the investment. Jesus Himself did not seek a reputation; on the contrary, He "made Himself of no reputation . . . and became obedient unto death, even the death of the cross." (Phil. 2:7-8).

Fame is perishable. The heroes of today are forgotten tomorrow, and their prestige often dies with their generation. Lives that are not invested for eternal values become statistics in an almanac. If statues are erected to their memory, the next generation simply inquires, "Who's that?"

2. *Power.* Another prize many people seek, and for which they sell their lives, is power. To obtain seats of authority, they will sacrifice time, friends, property, and integrity. The

opportunity to play chess with other men's lives, to sway the fate of nations, becomes an irresistible passion. The scandal of Watergate in the politics of the United States showed that absolute power can be a major temptation to those who possess some power, and that its misuse ultimately brings shattering calamity.

Mussolini, who intended to become another Caesar, was finally strung up by the heels on a gibbet, the victim of the fury of an incensed mob. Hitler, who almost conquered Europe, died in the bunkers of Berlin, forsaken by his associates. They gained what they wanted, but found that it had no permanent value.

3. *Possessions.* While wealth will buy almost anything that is material, it is still ephemeral, and cannot really satisfy the human heart. How can a personality that was made for eternity be satisfied with things that belong only to time? Money will not buy forgiveness of sins; it cannot insure the love of friendship; nor does it give assurance of life beyond death.

> The hour draws near, howe'er delayed and late,
>   When at th'eternal gate
> We leave the words and works we call our own,
>   And lift void hands alone
> For love to fill.
>   Our nakedness of soul
> Brings to that gate no toll;
>   Giftless we come to Him who all things gives,
> And live because He lives.

If these words sound pessimistic and depressing, it is not because prestige, power, and possessions are in themselves evil. Acclaim for good work done, the right to exercise authority within the sphere that God has given, and the possessions that provide the means for performing a lifework more effectively and easily, may all be just perquisites of a career pleasing to God. They are not, however, the main objective of life. And if they are so regarded, one may lose the most valuable thing of all—himself.

What Is the Loss of the Soul?

The soul is not a thing that can be lost as one might lose a purse or a bunch of keys; rather it involves the loss of life's meaning. To engage in a constant scramble for what is called success can become a dull and boring routine. If one fixes his attention on *prestige,* he is never satisfied with what he does attain. He must always try to rise to another rung of the social ladder. Little by little he becomes so intent on climbing that he loses all sense of obligation to others. They become either obstacles on the road to fame or pawns that he can maneuver for his advantage, rather than persons to whose development he can contribute.

Judas Iscariot is a classic example of one who lost his soul in that struggle. He was so intent on a prominent place of power that he had no sympathy for the sacrifice of devotion in Mary's gift of ointment to Jesus. He characterized her offering of love to Jesus as waste! In the contest for prestige, Judas lost his soul by his callousness, by his dishonesty, and by his selfish treachery (John 12:3-6). Life for him had ceased to be a joy—it had become a mania. All consciousness of obligation and all sense of loyalty had been eclipsed by the passion for self-exaltation.

Power can intoxicate. An extreme example in modern days is Idi Amin, the sergeant who made himself dictator of a nation. Its revenues were used for his aggrandizement; its people became his slaves; his imagined opponents were massacred or driven into exile, sometimes barely escaping with their lives. Finally, he was forced out of power, and relegated to obscurity. His misuse of rulership brought the deterioration of his own character and the development of a bestial cruelty scarcely exceeded in the annals of history.

Possessions are no sure guarantee of comfort and satisfaction. Only as they are used for the benefit of others do they take on value. That value depends not merely on their material, workmanship, or purchasing power, but upon the effect they produce in those who possess them. Art is of value only when it affects the minds and spirits of those who appreciate it; houses have value only as they provide for the health and efficiency and happiness of those who inhabit them; and stocks and bonds are merely printed paper except as they represent income to support life. None of these things can constitute life itself.

George Eastman was a young inventor who became interested in photography. He devised a means of simplifying the art of taking pictures and produced the Kodak camera with rolls of film that were easily portable and convenient to use. Capitalizing on the growing hobby of taking pictures, he built a flourishing business and amassed a fortune. He is reputed to have given $100 million to philanthropic and educational programs. Needless to say, he accumulated wealth for himself, and one might suppose that he would have been a happy man. In later life he became ill, and finally committed suicide. His property could not buy him health or peace of mind. To live only for what the world can give is not a good deal. The personality of man cannot be traded profitably for prestige, power, or possessions.

What Is the Best Deal?

The life of Jesus Himself is the answer to the question, although at first it seems like a contradiction of all good sense and practical wisdom. He was born in an obscure village of a remote province that was held in contempt by its neighbors (John 1:46). He belonged to a race that was generally disliked and scorned by the population of the Roman Empire. He had no classical education nor did He have any professional or business training. He was probably the village carpenter. His only property consisted of the clothes that He wore. He had no home of His own. When he wanted money, He had to borrow it. He embarked upon a ministry that was not underwritten by any board and had no distinguished supporters. He devoted His energies to healing the sick, comforting the sorrowing, and teaching the ignorant. He made many powerful enemies by exposing hypocrisy and by rebuking injustice. Finally, He was captured by His opponents, was condemned on false charges, and was executed ignominiously.

Probably by most of our modern standards, He would have been called a failure. Nevertheless, His words still live and are the most potent force for righteousness in the modern world. The integrity of His personal character transcends the deprecatory sneers of the cynic and the false evaluations of the ignorant. His cruel and shameful death became the means of man's reconciliation with God, because He atoned for the sins of a humanity that rejected Him. He invested His life in humiliation to the point of death, and God exalted Him by raising Him to enduring and triumphant life. He exemplified in Himself the best deal that one can make. To use His phraseology, "Except a grain of wheat fall into the ground and die, it abideth alone; but if it die, it bringeth forth much fruit" (John 12:24).

Let it be clear that the investment of personality is not synonymous with asceticism. There is no virtue in abusing one's body by starvation or by wearing hair shirts, as did many of the hermits and monks of the early Christian centuries. They thought that they were earning merit for salvation by so doing; but salvation cannot be gained by that method. However, this does not mean that we should avoid hardship, if it is incidental to accomplishing a task. Neither suffering nor comfort can be an end in itself. The one important consideration is to invest one's energies, intellect, and emotional outreach in such a way as to gain the greatest profit when viewed from the vantage of eternity.

For this kind of commitment, there is no index of values such as may be found in the market quotations of *The Wall Street Journal*. No stereotyped form is available. Each life must be invested for God in the way and place that He prescribes. He must be given full control of its desires and destinies, and must be allowed to direct its development.

What Does This Investment Mean?

The author of the Epistle to the Hebrews addressed a group of people who, because of their avowed faith in the Lord Jesus Christ, had suffered greatly. They had been exposed to ridicule and reproach, and robbed of their just possessions. To encourage them, he wrote: "Cast not away, therefore, your confidence, which hath great recompense of reward. For ye have need of patience that, after ye have done the will of God, ye might receive the promise. . . . But we are not of them who draw back unto perdition; but of them that believe to the saving of the soul" (Heb. 10:35-39). Following this exhortation is the eleventh chapter of Hebrews, which contains a long roll of men and women who did persist in their faith, thereby gaining the completeness of life that God had planned for them. They chose the best deal.

1. *Committing.* To choose the best deal means, first of all, a sincere commitment of oneself to Christ. Salvation is more than what God does *for* us, important as that is; it is also something done *with* us. The two are inseparable; for if He has redeemed us from slavery to our sins and has forgiven us for our past transgressions, we are indebted to Him for His goodness; and we ought to be amenable to those changes that He desires to effect in us, so that we may serve Him effi-

ciently and acceptably. To invest our lives in the purpose of God brings the fullest possible development and the greatest returns of which we are capable.

In dealing with God, we are not bargaining shrewdly with one who is trying to extract as much from us as possible for the least that He can give to us. Jesus lived in a country where business was conducted by trading rather than by a fixed price system. The same bargaining system prevails today in the Oriental world. On one occasion I strolled into a store in old Jerusalem where the owner had coins for sale. At first I had little interest in what he exhibited, until he produced a Jewish silver shekel of the First Revolt, minted A.D. 69, the last year before the fall of Jerusalem. That coin is rather rare, and would have been a prize. He set the price at $180. I demurred, assuring him that I did not have that amount to spend. Then he offered me a similar coin of the previous year, which is not so rare, and asked $80 for it. I thanked him for his efforts to please me, but said that such a price was still too expensive for me. He inquired what I would give for it. Realizing that even half that price would be more than I could afford, I assured him that I did not wish to insult him by offering less than it was worth, and concluded that I would have to forego the purchase. As I started to walk out of the store, he called me back and said, "I want you to have this coin. What will you give me for it?"

I replied, "I hesitate to make an offer that is unfair, but since you have asked me for it, I can give you $10."

"It is yours," he said, and handed it to me. I had no intention of beating him down, but obviously he had paid less for the coin than what I offered.

2. *Receiving.* When we invest our all in Him, He pours into our lives the best that He has. He wants to give us more than we give to Him.

When we invest our lives in God's purpose, we do not lose

our souls, but, by implied contrast, save them. *Save* means not only rescue from destruction, but the development that results from constant growth and improvement. The very best deal that we can make is to put our resources at God's disposal and watch Him bring out of them more than we had ever expected. Latent abilities are brought into action; obedience to God's instruction brings unanticipated opportunities; and even discipline that seems painful at times produces a richer and more useful life. God never cheats us by giving less than we have dedicated to Him. He does not promise ease or luxury, but He does give fullness of joy and freedom from worry.

The man who has placed his money in a well-managed bank or who has purchased stock in a strong business feels secure because of his confidence in the institution to which he has entrusted his fortune. How much more secure can one feel when he puts his entire personality and his possessions in the hands of God, who never suffers from depressions and who has not gone bankrupt! And if the ultimate riches are the intangibles which we can take with us, how much better is this investment than the one which is subject to the fluctuations of varying political and economic conditions.

If the believer does not have all that the world seems to offer and which will perish with time, he can have more that God can offer and which endures to eternity. There is an old story of a wealthy man who died and was ushered into the other world by a being who told him that he would be conducted to his heavenly dwelling place. As they rode down the residential streets, the late deceased saw a luxurious house located on a small hill and wondered if it were his.

"No," said his guide, "that belongs to your janitor, and is waiting for him. He is a godly man and spent his life in serving others."

Somewhat farther along a very handsome estate came into view. "Is that mine?" the new arrival queried.

"No," came the answer, "that belongs to your washer-woman. On the pittance you paid her, she brought up her children to serve Christ, and supported some missionaries too."

They turned down another road into a part of the city that was poorly built, and stopped in front of a shack that was constructed of odds and ends of material. "This," said the guide, "is yours."

When the owner protested in shocked surprise that he had expected something better that would befit his station in life, the guide replied, "We did the best we could with what you sent ahead."

While this imaginative story does not illustrate all of the truths involved, the principle is valid. A believer's *destiny* does not depend upon his works, but upon the grace of God appropriated by faith. His *reward*, however, will be the outcome of his investment. When we stand before Christ,

"Every man's work shall be made manifest; for the day shall declare it, because it shall be revealed by fire; and the first shall test every man's work of what sort it is. If any man's work abide which he hath built upon it, he shall receive a reward. If any man's work shall be burned, he shall suffer loss; but he himself shall be saved, yet as by fire" (1 Cor. 3:13-15).

What sort of a deal are you making with your life? Is it for prestige? God will not inspect us for medals, but for the scars incurred in His service. Your present prestige will count for nothing.

Is it for power? Your temporal sceptre will vanish when you stand before the King of kings and Lord of lords; for before His judgment bar, the great and small all will be equal.

Is it for possessions? They will have been left behind you, for the coin of earth will not be legal tender in the eternal world. Only what has been invested in the service of Christ will be accounted valuable. For this reason, the Word of God speaks to us:

I beseech you therefore, brethren, by the mercies of God, that ye present your bodies a living sacrifice, holy, acceptable unto God, which is your reasonable service. And be not conformed to this world, but be ye transformed by the renewing of your mind, that ye may prove what is that good, and acceptable, and perfect, will of God. (Rom. 12:1-2).

That is the best deal this life can offer. Take it today! Tomorrow will be too late!

8
Do You Know Who I Am ?

When Jesus came into the borders of Caesarea Philippi, He asked His disciples, saying, "Who do men say that I, the Son of man, am?"

And they said, "Some say John the Baptist; some, Elijah; and others, Jeremiah, or one of the prophets." He saith unto them, "But who say ye that I am?"

Matthew 16:13-15, asv

As Jesus continued His ministry, He realized that a crisis was impending. Many factors contributed to it. The death of John the Baptist at the hands of Herod Antipas had revealed the danger of Herod's anger against any who criticized his actions or who seemed to be gathering a following. When Jesus learned of this tragedy, He assembled His disciples and withdrew to the east side of the Jordan River for a conference

91

(Matt. 14:13). When He was interrupted by a crowd who desired more teaching, there followed the occasion of the Feeding of the Five Thousand and their attempt to make Him king. Realizing that even the rumor of such a movement would instantly jeopardize Him with Herod Antipas, who was already suspicious (Matt. 14:1), He withdrew to the mountain to pray while the disciples returned to Capernaum (John 6:16-17). At the same time, the enmity of the Jewish religious authorities increased, and plots against His life were multiplying (John 7:1). Many of His own disciples were leaving Him, and He seemed to have some doubts about the Twelve who had been His close companions and the active core of His numerous followers.

In order to have a better opportunity to be free from interruptions while conferring with His disciples, He then led them to the town of Caesarea Philippi. The situation had become critical, and Jesus needed both to give the disciples further instruction and to elicit from them a committal of loyalty. He knew already what their action would be (John 6:70-71), but He wanted them to declare voluntarily what their reaction would be to Him and to the circumstances that He anticipated. Would they follow Him to the end of the road? Could He rely on them to maintain His work after He had gone? Would they have the persistent faith in Him that would survive His declining popularity and their shock at His rejection and death?

Since He would count on them to interpret and to perpetuate the message after He had left them, He wanted to know their intentions. Were they like the fickle crowd who wanted food, miracles, and entertainment, or had they seen in Him the revelation of God? Were they interested only in a venture that might make them powerful and free citizens of a new state, or had they fixed their faith in Him so that they would trust Him, even if their cherished dreams about Him were rudely shattered? It was a problem of leadership, and it fore-shadowed an internal crisis that must be met before He could confront the external one.

Two Questions—Three Answers

With this in mind Jesus probed them with two questions. The first was general: "Who do men say that I, the Son of man, am?" (Matt. 16:13) Mark stated it more personally, "Who do men say that I am?" (Mark 8:27) and Luke's version is like Mark's. This question did not call for an immediate commitment. Jesus was asking that they should define the popular concept of His ministry, in order that He might know how His person and message were being received.

Three answers were given. The first was that He was John the Baptist risen from the dead. The influence of John had been so widespread and so powerful that it seemed to many people that Jesus was simply a restoration or reincarnation of His predecessor. Herod Antipas, doubtless agitated by a guilty conscience, had such a concept of Him. There were resemblances between them. John had appeared suddenly without previous introduction, and Jesus had emerged on the scene without fanfare and advertising. Both preached a message of repentance in anticipation of entering the kingdom of God. Both demanded individual acceptance of truth and acknowledgment by submitting to baptism (John 3:22-24). To the casual observer, Jesus' ministry would appear to be a continuity with John's.

The disciples, however, must have observed a difference. John was avowedly a forerunner for another; Jesus spoke for Himself. John's ministry was preparatory; Jesus' ministry was final. John performed no miracles; Jesus' ministry was filled with them (John 10:41). John acknowledged Jesus as superior, and the disciple who wrote the fourth Gospel duly recorded this (John 3:28, 30).

The second answer narrowed the circle of identity. Some regarded Jesus as the reappearance of Elijah. The reason for this identification was presumably the prophecy of Malachi: "Behold, I will send you Elijah, the prophet, before the coming of the great and terrible day of the Lord; and he shall turn the heart of the fathers to the children, and the heart of the children to their fathers, lest I come and smite the earth with a curse" (Mal. 4:5-6). The coming of Elijah as the precursor of God's final judgment had been predicted, and any person who could duplicate the deeds of Elijah would be a likely candidate in the popular thinking for the fulfillment of the prophecy. Elijah had performed miracles of healing and of providing food for the hungry. He had controlled wind and weather by his prayers. He had made the presence of God real when he defied the prophets of Baal on Mt. Carmel and had moved the whole nation back to God. There was ample demonstration of supernatural power in his life, as there was in the life of Jesus.

On the other hand, Elijah had spoken of the God of Israel as a great and powerful God, but not as his Father. Elijah had fled in a moment of discouragement and had begged God to take away his life, for he was no better than his fathers (1 Kings 19:1-8). He had taken orders and had fulfilled them as a servant.

In the face of danger, Jesus had maintained a consistent ministry, and had spoken of God in far more intimate terms. He did not fit the prophecy of Malachi in that He came to announce "the acceptable year of the Lord" (Luke 4:19) and not the hour of final judgment.

The disciples quoted one more rumor about Christ, that He was "Jeremiah, or one of the prophets." Jeremiah was the prophet of the Exile who had resided in Jerusalem prior to the devastation of the city by the army of the Babylonians and the ensuing removal that swept so many of the people into captivity. Perhaps Jeremiah's faithfulness to his message in spite of official repudiation and ridicule, and his compassionate anguish for the fate of the people caused the populace to liken Jesus to him. Jeremiah had suffered obloquy and persecution, and had not retracted one word of his message. Jesus had followed the same pattern. However, there was no promise that Jeremiah would return from the dead, and the utterances of Jesus were neither political in character nor as pessimistic in tone as were Jeremiah's. The disciples did not affirm this rumor either; and they added that the multitude was uncertain, saying that He might be one of the prophets.

All of these answers indicated that the public recognized His unusual powers; they also implied both astonishment and respect. To any person seeking popularity, they would have been encouraging; but Jesus was not conducting a popularity contest. During His ministry up to this point, He had concealed or repressed the idea of Messiahship as the populace conceived it, and had refused to permit any suggestion that He be elevated to public office (John 6:15). He was desirous of discerning acceptance, not of superficial applause.

"But Who Say Ye That I Am?"

No permanent discipleship can be built on so shaky a foundation as a passing opinion or a piece of theological guesswork. Jesus wanted the disciples to evaluate Him more profoundly and personally. In order to elicit such a confession, He probed the disciples even more deeply: "But who say *ye* that I am?"

1. *Serious evaluation.* The question demanded first of all that the disciples evaluate Him seriously. Like the general public, they were attracted to Him by various motives. Some saw in Him a potential leader who could unite the discordant elements in Judaism and lead them to that realization of their patriotic hopes—an independent state under a theocratic

government. Their interests were political and economic. Some accepted Him as a teacher whose novel presentation of truth and imperative ethics stirred their minds and consciences. Others realized that He was unique, and though He mystified them by the parables and sayings whose meaning often eluded them, they responded to friendship with love and devotion. He desired an intelligent and clear understanding of His person and work, so that they would become loyal disciples. He wanted them to progress from an experimental investigation to an assessment that would entail obligation. If they valued Him supremely, they would be willing to commit their lives to the values that He had established.

Growing knowledge always calls for decisions of greater scope and consequence. Each such decision may contain the germ of the next one, yet each is distinct as a step of progress. The boy who receives Christ as his Saviour is aware that a new Person has entered his life in whom he trusts for his final salvation, and whom he follows as his present Leader. Later he may confront the issue as to whether the Leader shall decide what his career shall be. If he accepts that decision, then the next one may well be what sort of training he shall choose to carry out the preceding decision. At each stage there will be an enlarging consciousness of the nature of Christ and of His will for the individual.

2. *Personal confession.* The question could not be answered by custom or by acquiescence as a member of a community or by a majority vote. It called for a personal confession. Relation with Christ can never be purely institutional. Up to this time, the disciples had looked upon Jesus as somebody who could fulfill their hopes. Even later, looking back at the crucifixion, the two bewildered men on the road to Emmaus said to Jesus, "We *hoped* that it had been He who should have redeemed Israel" (Luke 24:21). To them Jesus' death had closed the possibility of His ever accomplishing

what they had expected. They had joined His company and had, like the others, looked to Him for certain results because of a common concept that He would become the Messianic liberator of His nation. But they had not understood His real purpose, though He had explained it on numerous occasions. The sacrificial and eternal aspects of His ministry had not dawned on them.

An answer to His question cannot be settled by joining a general consensus of opinion or by affiliation with an institution. There must be a definite statement of one's own verdict concerning Him. It presupposes careful thought and a final conclusion. Jesus did not desire compliance with a majority action, nor a momentary emotional reaction. He wanted a reasoned, though not unfeeling, independent response.

3. *Personal commitment.* To admit a truth is not to commit oneself to it. One may be convinced by logic or won by a demonstration, and still not be willing to act upon what is conceded to be right. There is need for personal commitment.

When Blondin, a famous acrobat, visited America, he demonstrated his skill on the tightrope by performing on a cable suspended over Niagara Falls. He carried a stool and a small table with a cup and saucer on it out to the middle of the cable, balanced them and himself on them, and enjoyed a cup of tea. Then he returned, loaded a wheelbarrow with brick, trundled it across the Falls on the cable, and brought it safely back. The audience watched him with astonishment, and applauded him vigorously. Then he turned to one of the men on the bank of the river and said, "Do you believe that I can push a heavy load across the river in the wheelbarrow, and back?"

"Sure," came the reply. "I saw you do it."

"Very well. Get in the wheelbarrow and I will take you across."

"Oh no! Not I!"

Did the man really believe Blondin or not? If he had believed to the point of commitment, he would have accepted the offer.

One can intellectually believe in a correct theology about Jesus and still not be a genuine believer. He can agree that Jesus was supernatural, and yet not be willing to bear a cross. Even more than their confidence in His claims, Jesus wanted the companionship of the disciples in His sufferings. He said to them at the Last Supper, "Ye are they who have continued with Me in My trials" (Luke 22:28); and in Gethsemane he challenged Peter, who had fallen asleep from fatigue: "What, could ye not watch with Me one hour?" (Matt. 26:40) While Jesus' question to the disciples asked for an evaluation, it also involved a commitment.

"Thou Art the Christ"

Peter's answer expressed his decision, and apparently that of the disciples. When Andrew first summoned his brother to meet Jesus, he said that he had "found the Messiah, which is, being interpreted, the Christ" (John 1:41). On that occasion Peter made no profession of anything, but it must have started a train of thought in his mind. He associated himself with Jesus, traveled with Him (John 2:2, 12), lent Him his boat for a pulpit (Luke 5:4), witnessed Jesus' healing of his mother-in-law (Matt. 8:14-15), and had ample opportunity to observe many other miracles and to listen to His teachings.

This confession, "Thou art the Christ (Messiah), the Son of the living God," revealed that Peter had considered carefully all that Jesus was and did, and that he had arrived at a studied conclusion. It was not a snap judgment. Admittedly, Peter failed to measure up to his own commitment, but his sincerity in making it was unimpeachable, and he never relinquished it. It became a fixed point of achievement in his spiritual progress and presumably was such for the others as well, although their individual replies are not recorded here. The effect of this confession was fourfold.

1. Inauguration. The confession was an affirmation to which the disciples must adhere. It was like the signing of a contract. When one is negotiating a sale, there is always a period in which the customer may inspect the goods, make comparisons of costs and qualities, bargain if necessary on price, and consider whether the object for sale will meet his needs. At some point, however, he must sign the agreement to purchase. When he decides, he is committed to take delivery of the goods and to pay for them. Jesus' question involved more than obtaining a casual opinion. It was a landmark crisis that settled the status of Peter and the others as His disciples, and that inaugurated the new life which they would experience with Him. At least, this one was climactic and irrevocable.

2. Inviolate commitment. Such a decision is imperative for a genuine Christian experience. Nothing lasting or real can be accomplished by an uncommitted life. Christian commitment may be compared to marriage, in that one is either married or he is not. The reason for a wedding is that the young couple should make irrevocable pledges to each other upon which their family life can be founded. If the pledges are not kept, disaster follows. Of course, the commitment should be made on the basis of complete investigation and confidence; but once made, it should be kept inviolate. In discipleship Christ makes His claims upon us continually, and stretches our faith by new tests as time passes. These things, however, should not be regarded as contradictory to our initial knowledge of Him, but should rather be interpreted as part of a growing comprehension of His character and purpose. They introduce us to further experience of the same Person in whom we placed our first confidence.

The commitment is therefore the beginning of a new learning process. When Peter made his confession at Caesarea Philippi, Jesus immediately introduced him to the idea that the Son of man must suffer before entering into His glory (Luke 9:22-26). Both were equally certain in the program of establishing His kingdom. Jesus elaborated it by saying, "The Son of man must suffer many things, and be rejected by the elders and chief priests and scribes, and be slain, and be raised the third day" (v. 22). This announcement must have shocked the disciples, who would have wondered what sort of reward there would be for the sacrifice of all that they held dear—their families and homes, their careers and their futures. Then Jesus added, "If any man will come after Me, let him deny himself, and take up his cross daily, and follow Me" (v. 23). Peter himself learned what Jesus meant as he underwent the suffering that his subsequent service for Christ occasioned. He spoke in his first epistle of "the sufferings of Christ, and the glory that should follow" (1 Peter 1:11), and commented that we were "called" to partake of them because "Christ also suffered for us, leaving us an example, that ye should follow His steps" (2:21). He suggested that we should have the attitude of Christ toward this suffering, and even rejoice in it (4:1, 13). This process of learning, however, would not all be suffering, for the Lord had promised glory which would be the final reward for the disciples (5:1, 10). The process of learning by hard experience brings at the end the satisfaction of a victory well won.

3. *Expanding commitment.* Enlarging experience brings an expanding commitment. As we enter into new tasks and problems, we soon realize that we become more dependent on Christ and consequently more closely united to Him than ever before. To revert to the figure of marriage, the initial commitment is not necessarily jeopardized by the strains and sorrows that occur later. As the spouses overcome those perils

by meeting them together, the mutual bond of love and confidence can be strengthened.

4. *Risk-taking.* To follow Christ means entering upon new and unfamiliar territory, to take increasing risks for Him, and to trust Him fully in more difficult circumstances. Each new decision involves severer tests. At the time when this question was asked, the disciples had followed Him through ridicule and attack; they had acted as His agents in ministry where they were subjected to the same pressures that He endured, and they had been faithful. They had already followed, but they still had a long distance to go.

Expectation

There was, however, an ultimate terminus. The answer to this question evoked the disclosure of an eschatological expectation: "For whosoever shall be ashamed of Me and of My words, of him shall the Son of man be ashamed, when He shall come in His own glory, and in His Father's and of the holy angels" (Luke 9:26). As Peter remarked in his first epistle, the long pathway of following Christ could end only when He took the crown that is rightfully His. The appearance of the incandescent Christ in the Transfiguration was the sample of what Peter's confession would ultimately mean.

The full significance of confessing Jesus as the Messiah of God is that it brings us into an expanding relationship with Him which ends in glory. The pilgrimage may be arduous, but the destination makes it worthwhile. St. Stephen the Sabaite, who learned this lesson, expressed it in this poem:

"If I find Him, if I follow,
  What His guerdon here?"
"Many a sorrow, many a labor,
  Many a tear."

"If I still hold closely to Him
What hath He at last?"
"Sorrow vanquished, labor ended,
Jordan passed."

"Finding, following, keeping, trusting,
Is He sure to bless?"
"Saints, apostles, prophets, martyrs
Answer YES!"

9
Are You Leaving Me Too ?

"You do not want to leave too, do you?" Jesus asked the Twelve. John 6:67, NIV

There is an emotional pathos in this question that reveals instantly the mind of Jesus. It was spoken to His disciples at the turning point of His career. This question as recorded by John differs from the synoptic narratives in Matthew 16, Mark 8, and Luke 9, in that it reveals more of Christ's personal feeling. The previous question, about who men considered Him to be, involved a verdict on His character and mission which might have been rendered rather impersonally. The grammatical structure of this question, however, presupposes that the answer of the disciples should be negative. Many English translators do not make this difference clear. The King James Version renders the text, "Will ye also go away?" To be sure, the word *also* implies that He expected more of the Twelve than of the peripheral group who were not so intimately attached to Him, but it could have been answered yes or no without violating an expected sequence. The Greek particle that introduces the question, however, indicates that He expected a strong negative reply: "No, we do not want to leave you."

The Context

The situation that evoked this question was related more to the actions of the public than to rumors of their opinions. Subsequent to the Feeding of the Five Thousand, there were two events that affected the popular reaction. The first was Jesus' refusal to accept the leadership of a revolutionary cause. The crowds that had witnessed the miracle and had benefited by it were so excited that they wished to seize Him and make Him king (John 6:15). Their desire was to have a ruler who could supply all their material needs miraculously. He would be able to inaugurate a regime in which everybody would be fed gratis, without the hard labor and economic pressure under which they were living. Everybody likes to receive something for nothing, and the prospect of perpetually free lunches naturally appealed to them.

Furthermore, a person who could exercise such miraculous powers would be an invincible political leader. Why should they fear the legions of Rome if He could wither them by a word of command or by a mere gesture? Surely, they thought, this man was "the prophet" who should come into the world. Perhaps He would be like Elijah, who had called down fire from heaven and who could reform and restore the nation overnight. Jesus, however, declined to accept any such position, and withdrew to the mountain to pray. He was sensitive to the Father's will, and already had a knowledge of God's purpose for the time. He had not come to take the leadership of a local revolution, even for Israel, but rather to become the Saviour of the world. When He would not leave His objective to serve their rash desires, the crowd abandoned Him.

The second event was Jesus' application of His purpose into teaching that bewildered and alienated them. It was an early demonstration of "the offense of the Cross" (Gal. 5:11). His preaching in the synagogue of Capernaum did not deal with national politics but with personal faith. He said, "I am the Living Bread that came down from heaven; if any man eat of this bread, he shall live forever. . . . Verily, verily, I say unto you, 'Except ye eat the flesh of the Son of man, and drink His blood, ye have no life in you'" (John 6:51-53). These words implied that faith must be centered in His person rather than in His powers; that He was necessary to their spiritual life as the bread which He multiplied for them was to their physical life; and that He must become a part of their life as bread is absorbed into the fabric of the body.

The effect of His preaching was a negative public reaction. The people recoiled from the concept of eating His flesh, for they perceived only the literal statement, and said, "How can this Man give us His flesh to eat?" (v. 52) To them His words seemed crassly irrational and incomprehensible. Jesus explained that He was talking about abiding in Him, and afterward explained to the disciples that He was speaking figuratively of spiritual matters. His hearers still did not comprehend His meaning, and did not believe.

While this event may not be identical with that of Caesarea Philippi, it is generally parallel to it both in time and in significance. In both instances the attitude and action of the populace are reflected. The imminence of Jesus' approaching death is indicated and the reaction of the disciples is described in similar terms. The concern of Jesus is presented in both by the questions that He asked, though in John's Gospel, the discussion seems to have been largely public, whereas in the Synoptics, it was a private experience.

The Concern

Baffled by the mysterious metaphor of eating His flesh and drinking His blood, and disappointed by His refusal to accept the role that the crowd had tried to thrust upon Him, many of the disciples turned back to their usual occupations and "walked no more with Him" (v. 66). The pathos of Jesus' question shows that He was more troubled by losing them than by the apparent failure of His enterprise. Each disciple who deserted Him was an object of His love, and He did not want to bid them farewell.

The person of Christ as portrayed in the Gospels is not a remote or legendary object of worship, serving merely as a framework for an intricate theology. Neither is He like the Buddha, "calm, passionless, at peace." His life was wrapped up with the people whom He had called to follow Him; and as they left Him one by one, He suffered a pang of sorrow. As these peripheral disciples melted away into the distance, He turned to the Twelve and inquired poignantly, "You do not want to go away too, do you?"

Jesus was contrasting the obvious failure of the majority with His expectancy for the Twelve. Up to this time, they had been willing to follow Him anywhere; would they also persevere on the last lap of His perilous journey? He was well aware of Peter's wavering temperament, of Thomas' skepticism, of Philip's materialism, and of the shortcomings of the others. Notwithstanding these faults, He loved them and could not bear to part with them.

This one short question reveals the depth of Jesus' love for the disciples. He had chosen them and called them, and had put confidence in them. As He said later, "Ye have not chosen Me, but I have chosen you" (John 15:16). As His personal and private selections, they were dear to Him. Although He must have been inwardly assured of their persistent loyalty, He questioned them in order to evoke from them some expression of their feeling for Him. Here the uncertainty of humanity and the purpose of deity intersected, as he disclosed to them His inner longing for sympathy and comradeship.

The evident overtone of Jesus' question foreshadowed the increasing loneliness that would envelop Him as He approached the cross. He was lonely because He was not understood even by His best disciples. They were not hostile, but they had no real comprehension of the strain under which He was laboring, or of the purpose that He was seeking to fulfill. The leaders of the nation had repudiated Him as a lawbreaker and an apostate (John 9:16; 10:33). His brothers did not believe in Him (John 7:5).

The disciples could not fathom His anguish for the city of Jerusalem, which was doomed to judgment for its sins (Luke 19:41-44). Their blind concern for their own advancement, at the time He was confronted with death, prevented any expression of sympathy for Him. Even in Gethsemane the foremost trio of the group fell asleep instead of praying with Him. He had to tread the winepress alone, for they were unprepared to stand with Him.

The wording of Jesus' question reveals also an expectation of their affirmative response. Jesus was certain that they would not fail to measure up to the challenge that He had given. The crowd had deserted Him because He would not conform to its demands; but He anticipated a different response from these men who had known Him intimately. He had even given the benefit of the doubt to Judas, of whose final perfidy He was painfully conscious (John 6:70-71). Perhaps this was more indicative of Jesus' faith in the Father than in them. In His subsequent prayer prior to Gethsemane, He said, "I have manifested Thy name unto the men whom Thou gavest Me out of the world; Thine they were, and Thou gavest them to Me" (John 17:6). Coupled with the statement from an earlier discourse—"My Father, who gave them to Me, is greater than all, and no man is able to pluck them out of My Father's hand" (John 10:29)—Jesus' words show that He had committed them to the Father, and was certain that ultimately they would be with Him in the Father's house. They might waver, but they would not be lost to Him.

This combination of concern and of certainty is representative of Christ's attitude toward all the disciples. In it lies the basis for the confidence of the believer that his salvation is unshakable. There is, on the one hand, the deep solicitude of our Lord for our loyalty and fellowship, both of which He desires. On the other hand, He expects from us a favorable response. It is a sobering thought that our attitudes and actions have become a matter of personal concern to Him. His redemption is not an impersonal transaction like a commercial deal. It is the expression of a love that has assumed the responsibility of forgiving our weaknesses and sins in order to unite us with Himself. Those who reject Him are not dismissed coldly, but are relinquished with deepest regret and sorrow.

Judas, the one who failed to meet Jesus' expectation of the Twelve, was not repudiated publicly by Jesus, even on the occasion of his treachery. At the Last Supper, Jesus handed Judas the morsel of food which normally conveyed the implication of special friendship (John 13:26); and when he appeared in the Garden with the armed company to make the arrest, Jesus did not berate him, but said reproachfully, "Judas, betrayest thou the Son of man with a kiss?" (Luke 22:48) The negligence and perversity of men is a grief to God; and though His judgments are sure, He administers them with reluctance. It is this seemingly contradictory tension which was present on the cross.

The Confession

The response to Jesus' question was offered by Simon Peter (John 6:68). First, he reaffirmed the allegiance of the Twelve by the title *Lord*. Although it can be simply a polite title like *Mr.*, on this occasion it must have conveyed the acknowledgment of Jesus' command over their lives and fortunes. They would not repudiate Him, but would recognize His sovereignty. Jesus' implication that He expected more from them brought a strongly affirmative answer. The same principle has been adopted in commerce, as exemplified by the advertising slogan of Standard Oil: "You expect more from Standard, and you get it." Jesus did not raise the question as an accusation of hesitant loyalty, but as an encouragement to final resolution. It stimulated the best in Peter's attitude toward Jesus, and it is noteworthy that in subsequent answers to Jesus' questions, he used the same term (John 21:15-17). Even when he remonstrated against a command, he still acknowledged the lordship of Jesus (Acts 10:14) and obeyed Him.

The second part of Peter's reply expressed his awareness of the uniqueness of Jesus. "To whom shall we go? Thou hast the words of eternal life." He had compared Jesus with the religious leaders that he knew, and was convinced that Jesus alone could supply the key to eternal life.

Eternal life was defined by Jesus Himself: "And this is life eternal, that they might know Thee, the only true [real] God, and Jesus Christ, whom Thou hast sent" (John 17:3). Eternal life, then, is not to be measured by a span of existence, but by profundity of experience. Experience is determined by contact, for the wider one's contacts, the richer the possibilities for his life will be. A miner whose life is restricted to digging in a dark tunnel, and who seldom meets others whose occupation is different from his own, will never enjoy the full and varied life of a man who has the advantage of wide acquaintance with people of different occupations, of extended travel to other lands and cultures, and of high intellectual stimulus. Furthermore, quality of life is influenced by the character of the persons one meets and by the interest of the things observed. The better the persons and the objects, the fuller one's life should be.

To know God, who is the greatest Person of the universe, and to observe the wonders of His creation will constitute the highest kind of life. In order to know Him, one will need unlimited opportunity, since His personality cannot be comprehended after a few brief interviews. An eternity will be necessary for only a beginning of such acquaintance.

Probably Peter did not have all these ideas in mind when he made his affirmation, but they followed logically. He did realize that within the circle of his contemporaries, Jesus had no equal. He had revealed to His disciples a world that they did not know existed. His ethics were stricter than the Law yet more comprehensive, and devoid of legalistic complications. His teaching was profound, yet different from that of the religious leaders of His day because it was free from speculation. His life was consistent with His words, and even His enemies conceded that He was free from sin. His knowledge of God was not theoretical, but experiential. The scribes and the Pharisees were didactic; He was redemptive. Nobody else spoke with His authority or certainty. Why should the disciples leave Him for another?

Then Peter came to his final verdict: "We believe and know that You are the Holy One of God" (6:69, NIV). The two verbs *believe* and *are* are in the perfect tense which denotes an accomplished action resulting in a fixed state. Peter's expression could be paraphrased, "We have come to a settled belief and a complete realization. . . ." The disciples' belief was not simply the single affirmation of a moment, but a settled and abiding conviction. Their knowledge was not just a flash of instant perception, but the permanent awareness of a reality. Even though they might on occasion fall short of the truth to which they had subscribed, the foundation of their faith was sure: Jesus was indeed the Holy One of God.

Curiously enough, this title appears rarely in the New Testament. Peter, preaching to the assembly of the Jewish elders in Jerusalem, accused them of denying "the Holy One and the Just" (Acts 3:14), and John spoke of an "unction from the Holy One" (1 John 2:20), which may refer to the Holy Spirit whom Jesus sent to the disciples. It was also used by a demoniac, who thus paid compulsory homage to Jesus by submitting to His power (Mark 1:24).

The distinctive use of the title in the Old Testament occurs in Psalm 16:10: "Neither wilt Thou permit Thine Holy One to see corruption." This text was applied to Jesus by Peter on the Day of Pentecost (Acts 2:27) and by Paul in addressing the synagogue at Antioch in Pisidia (13:35). Elsewhere it appears frequently in the prophecy of Isaiah as a title of God Himself (1:4; 5:19; 12:6), or as applied to another personage called "the Redeemer of Israel" (Isa. 41:14; 43:14; 44:6; 49:7). Peter's application of this title to Jesus presupposed a very high view of His place before God, and parallels the declaration given in the synoptic Gospels, "the Christ of God." Peter recognized that Jesus was a sacred Person, worthy of his worship and adoration because He partook of the holiness of God Himself.

Jesus praised Peter for his affirmation of faith, even though He was aware of the weakness of the disciples, and we knew that in the crisis at Gethsemane, they would all forsake Him and flee. He did predict Judas' perfidy without naming Him, but there is no mention of inquiry on the disciples' part for the identity of the traitor. His words did not go unnoticed or they would not have been preserved; but their meaning seems not to have penetrated the minds of the disciples at that time.

They declared their positive faith in Jesus, and took their stand with Him. In spite of their misunderstanding and ignorance of His real objective, they maintained their intention of loyalty. To that extent the confession demonstrated courage. They could not know precisely what the future might hold, but they were sure that it would not be pleasant.

"You do not want to go away too, do you?" Peer presure is heavy and sometimes irresistible. We tend to go with the crowd; and while in the trivial things of life, that way may be acceptable, there are times when the opposite is necessary. Yet the choice should not be wholly negative. We choose against going with the crowd, not because of a sanctimonious obstinacy or of a desire to be "different," but because we do not want to leave Jesus alone. He has a calling to fulfill, and He longs to share it with us. As He said, "The works that I do shall [ye] do also" (John 14:12). He had a burden of prayer, and wanted the disciples to help Him bear it (Mark 14:33-34). He had a witness to carry to the world, and He commissioned them to assist Him (John 15:27). To us He says again, "You do not want to leave too, do you?"

It Is Always Too Early to Leave Him

Outside the gate of Rome on the Appian Way, which leads southward to the seaports, stands a building known as the Chapel of the Quo Vadis. It commemorates a legend about the Apostle Peter. When the persecution by Nero was at its height, Simon Peter was urged by the Christians to escape from the city. He complied with their insistence and was fleeing toward safety, when he saw a mysterious figure approaching him. As the person drew nearer, he recognized Jesus, and said to Him in Latin, "Quo vadis, Domine?"

Back came the answer: "I am going to Rome to be crucified again, because my servant Peter is leaving the church."

With tears of repentance and shame, Peter turned back to Rome, and went to his death. The chapel marks the place where the interview supposedly occurred.

It is always too early to turn away from Jesus. His message to the world is transmitted not by those who know about Him and leave Him, but by those who know Him and stay with Him. It may be that His teaching is incomprehensible, that His demands are intolerable, and that His aims are irrational. But where is there any other who can speak with His authority and who can exercise His power? To whom shall we go for help when we are threatened by failure? To whom shall we turn when the perplexities of life confuse us? To whom else can we pledge ourselves unconditionally without fear of disillusionment?

Whether we view life from our side as the fullness of experience that only He can offer, or from His side, as He seeks our loyalty to assuage His loneliness, there is no real alternative to Him. "He that hath the Son hath life; and he that hath not the Son of God hath not life" (1 John 5:12).

I've tried in vain a thousand ways
   My fear to quell, my hopes to raise;
Yet what I need, the Bible says,
   Is ever, only, Jesus.

He died, He lives, He reigns, He pleads;
   There's love in all His words and deeds;
There's all a guilty sinner needs
   Forevermore in Jesus.

Though some should sneer, and some should blame,
I'll go in all my guilt and shame,
I'll go to Him, because His name
   Above all names, is Jesus.

10
Have You Firsthand Information?

*Jesus answered him, "Sayest thou this thing of thyself, or
did others tell it thee of Me?"*   John 18:34

Pontius Pilate, the Roman prefect of Judea, had been roused
at an early hour by the urgent petition of the Jewish national
council to conduct a hearing for a prisoner whom they
deemed worthy of death. They would gladly have bypassed
Pilate had they dared to do so, but Roman law required that
only an official representative could administer a death penalty. So in the early hours of a Friday morning, they appeared
at the gate of his residence. They brought with them Jesus, on
whom they had already passed judgment, and asked Pilate to
confirm their verdict.

Pilate was not eager to do so. He intensely disliked the
official priesthood, since it had on several occasions refused to

bend to his will, and had made trouble for him at Rome. He probably felt that the priests had some scheme to promote, and he was not inclined to gratify them. Nevertheless, he had been appointed to adjudge such questions, and could not escape the responsibility. Realizing that action was unavoidable, he strode out into the courtyard, and opened the session by the routine question: "What accusation bring ye against this Man?" (John 18:29)

In a rather impudent manner, the crowd responded, "If He were not a malefactor, we would not have delivered Him up unto thee" (v. 30). Thinking that the case was purely a dispute over their national customs, he told them to settle it for themselves. Then they informed him that the prisoner was guilty of a capital crime, and that his verdict was necessary for execution.

Need for Decision

Pilate could not escape making the fateful decision. And this decision was momentous because the prisoner was Jesus. The accusation was treason: He was charged with claiming that He was King of the Jews. Any claim to be a king of a subject nation without advance consent by Rome would be prima facie evidence of treason, and Pilate knew it. So the trial began with the usual establishment of identity: "Art Thou the King of the Jews?" (v. 33)

To the surprise of Pilate, the prisoner did not answer with a simple yes or no, but with a question: "Sayest thou this thing of thyself, or did others tell it thee of Me?"

The governor was shocked. Who did this man think he was? He was supposed to answer questions, not to ask them. Furthermore, this Galilean from the obscure town of Nazareth was challenging the governor's authority to interrogate, by asking him if he were merely an agent for another. Pilate was furious. "Am I a Jew?" he retorted. "Your own nation and its leaders have put You on trial. What have You done?" (See v. 35.) Jesus' question was not intended as an insult. He spoke calmly and deliberately, not fearing the power of the judge. What He wanted to know was whether Pilate had adequate information concerning Him to render any judgment, positive or negative. Or was he acting merely on hearsay?

1. *Pilate's ignorance and Jesus' innocence.* If one can draw a correct deduction from the subsequent report of the conversation, Pilate knew little. He may have had some information from the high priest, Caiaphas, with whom Judas had previously made his arrangements. Never before had he met Jesus, and as the dialogue progressed, he found himself increasingly baffled by this Person who did not fear the might of Rome nor boast of Himself. He did not indulge in frenzied protestation, but maintained a quiet dignity. He did not appear patronizing, yet stated that anyone who loved the truth would listen to Him. The more Pilate heard, the more sure he was of Jesus' innocence, and the harder he struggled to acquit Him.

2. *Pilate's guilt and Jesus' guilelessness.* Before this strange person, Pilate found himself shackled by the chains of his own sins, and condemned by the penetrating gaze of One who was incarnate righteousness. The firsthand information that he acquired by contact was becoming his own condemnation. He began to wonder whether he or Jesus was on trial. The question implied, as did the entire interview, what the final human response to the ministry, character, and purpose of Jesus would be. Its implications reached far beyond the immediate occasion of that day in Pilate's praetorium. How Pilate answered it is now a matter of history, but how can it be answered today?

The question implies first of all that Jesus was willing to be interviewed seriously. He raised no objection to anyone who wished to investigate His credentials. The first disciples who made tentative inquiries concerning Him were welcomed to

His dwelling, and were able to satisfy their curiosity about His character and status (John 1:37-39). Even His enemies had been given opportunity to make contact with Him, for they frequently discussed with Him His power and His claims. When confronted by the high priest, He replied, "I spoke openly to the world; I even taught in the synagogue, and in the temple . . . and in secret have I said nothing" (John 18:20). If evidence were needed, it was available to anybody who would pay attention to it.

So it is today. The life and teachings of Jesus are accessible in the major languages of earth to all who can read. If they are unknown, it is not because they were intended only for a select few. The facts are obtainable in almost every quarter of the civilized world except where hostility or neglect have kept them from the people.

Decision from Firsthand Knowledge

Any important decision concerning Jesus should be made on the basis of firsthand knowledge. Theories can easily be found, and often they are logically constructed, but the related facts do not always support them. In the realm of science, experiments are accorded high value because conclusions are founded on evidence that is verifiable by repeated attempts.

1. Primary sources. In historical study, the greatest importance is attached to original documents and to interviews with participants in the events under discussion. Obviously, the events cannot be repeated on demand. Literary research depends on identifiable quotations for the support of conclusions. Primary sources are always the foundation for sound investigation. Certainly, any decisions which affect the spiritual life of man deserve a similar basis, since they affect all other aspects of his existence.

2. Accuracy. This information calls for accuracy. Every

surveyor knows that when he projects an angle in measuring land, a minute error in calculating the degrees on the scale of his theodolite can distort seriously the boundaries of the plot that he is laying out. The miscalculation of degrees on a compass will inevitably send a ship on the wrong course. Information concerning Christ must be drawn correctly before it is accepted as final. Each individual should investigate the evidence for himself.

3. *Prudent judgment.* The evidence must also be understood in relation to its setting. Pilate saw his prisoner as the problem of the moment. Jesus created a dilemma that needed to be solved for Pilate's personal convenience. If he acquitted Jesus on the grounds that He was not guilty of any legal offense against the government, the Jewish priesthood would be angry. Their report to the emperor would complicate further the tensions that had arisen because of Pilate's administrative errors, and would endanger his political future. If he ordered the execution of Jesus, he would violate all the principles of Roman justice and might bring down upon himself the vengeance of the Jewish God.

Pilate did not comprehend the statement of Jesus: "Everyone that is of the truth heareth My voice." Jesus implied that truth and justice are enduring, and that Pilate should act in accord with their eternal verities, rather than attempting to solve his own dilemma by some doubtful experiment. A halfway decision accomplishes nothing of permanent value. Jesus challenged Pilate to think more deeply and to discern exactly what the outcome of his decision might be. Pilate failed because his vision was too narrow. He saw only the need of extracting himself from political danger; he did not see the larger purpose of God. Hearsay does not provide a sound basis for spiritual decisions; personal knowledge is necessary.

Jesus' question was an appeal to Pilate's personal judgment. John's account of the interview stresses Jesus' interest in

Pilate. He looked on the Roman prefect not as a neutral official who was about to settle his case, but as a man whose
spiritual needs He could satisfy. He was able to understand
Pilate's political perils and the tensions that they created. He
was more concerned with Pilate's dilemma than with His own
fate, and He was endeavoring to elicit from him some statement that might open the way to a personal commitment.
What were Pilate's own sentiments at that moment? Was he
acting solely in accord with the reports brought by the high
priest and his colleagues, or was he making inquiry to satisfy
his own interests?

A casual survey of the trial of Jesus before Pilate leaves the
impression that Pilate had been involved only because of a
legal technicality. Had not Caesar's sovereignty decreed that
the power of inflicting the death penalty be lodged exclusively
with Roman magistrates, Jesus might never had been brought
before him. The Jewish council could have tried, condemned,
and executed Him without Pilate's knowledge or consent.
Since Pilate had to be the judge, he might well have regarded
the whole affair impersonally. In reality, the opposite proved
true. Pilate's wife was agitated, and begged her husband to
have nothing to do with the case (Matt. 27:19). Pilate realized
from the threat of the people that if he failed to gratify their
desire, they would report him to Tiberius as delinquent in his
duty (John 19:12). His personal fate was connected with Jesus.

Need Today for Firsthand Knowledge

The destiny of every living person is conditioned by his rela-
tion to Jesus. The alternative to listening to Him or ignoring
Him, to receiving Him or repudiating Him, to submitting to
Him or renouncing Him must be settled sooner or later.
There was no third alternative for Pilate, nor is there for us.

Because Jesus is a living Person, He can still be approached
by those who wish to learn of Him. He said to the crowds,

"Him that cometh to Me I will in no wise cast out" (John 6:37). No sincere seeker was ever turned away from Him because of his social, intellectual, or moral status. Hearsay may provide the first clue for contact, but earnest desire must carry the inquiry further.

Jesus is more than a contributor to the ethical wisdom of the human race; He is the pivot of destiny. He summons us to the bar of judgment and calls for a positive response. In order to make that response, we need firsthand knowledge. No verdict that we render will be worth anything unless it is supported by our personal acceptance of the facts and of His Person.

If the twelve apostles can be used as an index, the probability is that we would choose to follow Him after making an initial acquaintance. On the other hand, Judas was one of that number who had traveled in the company of Jesus, and had observed Him under all possible conditions. Yet he renounced Him at the last. Both acceptance and rejection were the outgrowth of firsthand knowledge.

To speak from personal experience means authenticity. Second-hand information may be correct; but one can speak with more assurance and with the ring of certainty if he has experienced what he says. A historian who describes a battle may do so vividly, but he can never compete with the veteran who was present on the field. The latter has witnessed the struggle and the carnage; he may bear the scars of the conflict; and the scene is stamped indelibly on his memory. He may not have known all of the factors involved or what transpired on other fronts; but he has no illusions about his own experience.

Reports concerning Jesus may be garbled or warped by the prejudices of the bearer. Imaginary concepts of what He is and of what He requires are often defective. Frequently, the flaws in His followers are assumed to be characteristic of Him, when actually the opposite is true.

A street preacher in England was being heckled by a man in the audience who ridiculed his message and scorned the Gospel which he proclaimed. Without saying a word, the preacher calmly pulled an orange from his pocket, peeled it, and ate it. Turning to his adversary, he asked the latter whether the orange were sour or sweet.

"You fool," said the heckler. "How can I tell? I never tasted it."

"Then," replied the preacher, "how do you know what Christ is like, since you have never experienced Him?"

A valid Christian experience must rest on firsthand knowledge; otherwise it will be too vague to be convincing, or else downright hypocritical. How can any person narrate what Christ has done for him unless he has first realized it inwardly?

Attaining Firsthand Knowledge

The first step to gaining this knowledge is often taken because of another person's witness of his relation to Christ. When his testimony is related sincerely and directly, others will wish to enjoy this relationship themselves. By conforming to the same principles that produced it in others, they may share in it themselves.

We see illustrations of this initial step of naked faith in many areas of life. I once bought a car of an unfamiliar make with no idea how it would perform. No acquaintance of mine owned one, but the price was right and it was sold by a reliable company. Now, having driven it for several thousand miles, I can assure anyone truthfully that it is a satisfactory car. It starts promptly in cold weather, has a low operating cost, and a comfortable ride. When somebody else asks about its performance, I can recommend it with assurance.

The second step is the maintenance of connection with

Christ. Christian experience cannot be estimated wholly on the basis of initial explosive ecstasy. The first awareness of forgiveness and freedom is thrilling, but will it last? It is for many people the normal beginning, but it is just the gateway to the reality of knowing Christ. For only after the passage of sufficient time do we perceive His defense against attack, His guardianship during temptation, and His comfort in sorrow. The progressive sense of His presence in daily life will bring that direct certainty that is needed. It will enable us to speak with confidence concerning Him.

Kipling, in his poem "Tomlinson," depicted the imaginary fate of a man who died, and who was refused entrance both to heaven and to hell because he could not merit either. His personal experience of both good and evil was secondhand, and consequently superficial and unreal. The last line of the poem reads, "The God you took from a printed book go with you, Tomlinson." Allowing for the fact that Kipling's theology was not orthodox, his poem does illustrate the truth that first-hand experience is demanded by God's judgment. At that final judgment bar, no one else can answer for us; we must speak for ourselves. Jesus' question put Pilate on the witness stand, and though he replied with a contemptuous dismissal, his real answer was evident. He was not interested in Jesus, but only in himself.

The opinions of others are an insufficient ground for an answer to Jesus' personal confrontation. He deserves a fair and honest answer. He is unwilling to accept evasions or compromises. He wants to deal directly with us as we are. Had Pilate not reacted with contempt but spoken from his heart, the story might have been different for him. He had his opportunity and lost it. What is your personal conviction concerning Jesus?

11
Where Is God Now ?

"My God, My God, why hast Thou forsaken Me?"

Mark 15:34

This tragic utterance, wrung from the lips of Jesus, is a strange enigma. It shocks us by its seemingly accusatory tone, as if Jesus were reproaching God for not having fulfilled His obligations. How was it possible that He who had maintained such unwavering trust in the goodness of God, and who had enjoyed unbroken intimacy of fellowship with Him, should suddenly feel that God had departed from Him?

One commentator has said that this is the hardest sentence in the Bible to explain. The complaint of Jesus seems utterly incongruous with the total orientation of His life. There is nothing like it in all of His previous teaching or remarks concerning God.

It is also unique in its application of Scripture. Jesus quoted from the opening of Psalm 22, which was presumably written by David. At what crisis in his career David composed these words is not known. It must have been at some point when he was deeply troubled because his enemies had surrounded him, and when he was exposed to physical suffering and public contempt. Strangely enough, it describes accurately the features of the crucifixion; the shame of exposure, the sarcastic ridicule of the mob, the distortion of the body, the intense thirst, the piercing of hands and feet, and the gambling for the victim's garments. This is even more remarkable because crucifixion was not a Jewish method of execution. Perhaps Jesus' use of the opening line of the Psalm indicated that He recognized it as a prediction of Himself, and thus an expression of His sufferings. He was claiming the prophecy as His own.

A Retreating Father?

This call to God was not phrased in the form by which Jesus usually prayed. Invariably He addressed God as *Father*. To Him God was not a distant deity, but an ever-present Companion on whom He relied for His very life and to whom He gave undeviating allegiance. When He stood at Lazarus' grave in Bethany, and in that breathless moment called on God to raise the dead man from the tomb, He said, "Father, I thank Thee that Thou hast heard Me" (John 11:41). The prayer of John 17, spoken only a few hours before the Cross, and with full understanding of His impending death, began with, "Father, the hour is come" (17:1). In the Garden of Gethsemane, as He awaited the arrival of the traitor who led the arresting party, He prayed, "Father, if it be possible, let this cup pass from Me" (Matt. 26:39). The sudden change in address revealed a corresponding change in attitude and relationship. While He did not repudiate God, He had clearly lost the sense of God's nearness and intimacy. He was suffering a darkness of the soul that had cut Him off from the very source of His life—a spiritual deprivaton that was more agonizing than even the physical suffering.

This aspect of the cry was an implied reproach. How could God leave Him? He had said of the Father, "I do always those things that please Him" (John 8:29). Jesus did not question God's dealing with Him, but accepted joyfully the Father's will as the directive for His work. Since He had always been obedient, why should the Father abandon Him in the hour of His extremity? It was impossible to conceive that God had voluntarily left Him; and yet, where was He?

Still another curious fact is that Jesus had not been overpowered by superior force. When Peter offered armed resistance to the posse that came to make the arrest, Jesus rebuked him and said, "Thinkest thou that I cannot now pray to My Father, and He shall presently give Me more than twelve legions of angels?" (Matt. 26:53). Jesus had accepted the suffering voluntarily and would not retract His decision. If, then, He had submitted to it, why should He question God for leaving Him?

Some have suggested that God had not really abandoned Him, but that Jesus, because of the anguish of the Cross, only thought that He had done so. Such a view does violence to the spiritual consciousness of Jesus. He was not dramatizing Himself nor playing for effect. He was not subject to self-deception. There was a real sense of God's withdrawal from Him to leave Him alone in the struggle. There was a gulf of darkness between Him and the Father such as He had never previously experienced. He neither desired nor deserved it.

A Mission of Identification

The strange anomaly of this episode must be explained in terms of His mission. From the beginning of His public career, He had identified Himself with the sins and sufferings of the human race. At His first appearance, when He presented Himself to John the Baptist as a candidate for baptism, the latter said, "I have need to be baptized of Thee, and comest

Thou to me?" (Matt. 3:14) Jesus' answer was, "Permit it to be so now, for thus it becometh us to fulfill all righteousness."

He took His place alongside of sinners in order that He might share their lot. Throughout His career He made Himself one with His disciples. He did not use His supernatural power to provide for Himself more food or shelter or rest than they had. He exposed Himself to public criticism and malicious opposition, and endured them meekly. With full knowledge of the plots of His enemies, "He steadfastly set His face to go to Jerusalem" (Luke 9:51). Perhaps His attitude is best expressed by His own statement: "The Son of man came, not to be ministered unto but to minister, and to give His life a ransom for many" (Mark 10:45). As He approached the climax of His ministry, He entered consciously into the sufferings that His mission entailed, and thus realized the anguish of a humanity that travels the same road and reaches its terminus with the consciousness of alienation from God.

Peter wrote of Christ's sufferings, that He "bore our sins in His own body on the tree, that we, being dead to sins, should live unto righteousness" (1 Peter 2:24). Sin inevitably brings adversity, alienation from God, despair, and death. Jesus willingly accepted our place that He might overcome these things for us, and that He might remove the obstacle that separated man and God. Therefore, He could not avoid participating in sin's disintegrating effect upon our human thinking, in the sense of severance from God, and in the hopelessness that accompanies death. If He were to represent us adequately, both in His atonement for sin and in His ability to minister to our daily needs, He must enter into the depth of experience that would make His work not an artificial device, but a genuine experience. How could He redeem sinners if He had not shared in their estrangement, or how could He deal with them convincingly if He had not felt their misery?

If Jesus knew that the Cross was unavoidable, why should

He question its accompaniments? Why did He not pay the price of accomplishing the mission without the cry of protest? The paradox of this episode illustrates the fact that suffering is no less painful because it is inevitable. Jesus was not a stoic who cultivated indifference to suffering because fate had decreed it. He was keenly affected by it, and asked for an answer to the problem. For Him it was answered by the Resurrection, which indicated that He had fulfilled all that God required of Him, and emerged triumphant from the test.

Routine, Futility, and Failure?

How does Jesus' question apply to our lives? To many of us, the despairing question is familiar because it expresses our feeling, when we are troubled by our misfortunes. As we realize our own insufficiency to cope with them, we cry out for God. Sometimes we are baffled by the seeming futility of life. Our occupations prove to be endless and dull routines from which we cannot escape, yet we make no progress toward our goals and have no hope of accomplishing anything that will have enduring value. From youth to age, we expand our struggles in profitless labor, and when we have finished, we have nothing to show for it.

If the career of Jesus were to be measured only by what He did until His death, it might have been regarded as futile. The disciples that He had gathered deserted Him in the Garden of Gethsemane, and of the two who followed Him to the trial, one denied Him and the other was unable to rescue Him. The crowds to whom He had ministered dispersed and forgot Him. He exercised no permanent influence on the official life of His nation. Nor did any of its leaders espouse His cause, except for two who took the responsibility of burying Him. He erected no building, inaugurated no political reforms, and no monuments were raised to His memory. In terms of worldly success, He seemed to have accomplished little. Yet the purpose of God transcended the apparent futility, and in spite of the overwhelming frustration of the Cross, He trusted God for the result. No life dedicated to God is ever useless.

Closely connected with the sense of futility is that of failure. How did Jesus feel about the results of His ministry? When He healed ten lepers, only one returned to thank Him. The effort expended on Judas did not deter him from becoming a traitor. All of Jesus' efforts to train Simon Peter culminated in his triple denial and subsequent shame. Jesus' miracles did not evoke faith in the majority of those who witnessed them, nor did His teachings win universal acceptance. His ministry did not produce a revival in Judaism, and certainly He was not publicly acclaimed throughout the world of His day. He was barely mentioned by the Roman historians, and then only as an insurgent executed by Pontius Pilate. If He contemplated the results of His labors only in the light of the moment, it is not surprising that He would feel that God left Him.

The sense of failure is dispiriting and depressing. It can paralyze activity and crush the spirit of the most enthusiastic adventurer. Jesus must have felt the same emotion that any one of us would have had under similar circumstances. To be sure, it passed away and did not alter His purpose, but it was there.

Where Was God?

Fear may have contributed to His anguish. Jesus was not a coward, for He had faced His enemies without shrinking and had given no sign of retreating or of surrendering to their demands. Nevertheless, the sense of being alone in the middle of opposition and the threat of death must have weighed upon Him. If God had left Him, what defense did He have against the weird and mysterious powers of evil?

Fear is not always a mark of a weak spirit. The greater

knowledge one has of danger, the greater will be his fear, but his resolution may match it. Courage is not always the absence of fear, but the strength of character that enables one to defy the danger and to overcome it. A veteran soldier knows well the threatening menace of his enemy, but boldly advances to the attack. Jesus was not naively ignorant of all that death could mean. As He was swept inexorably into its vortex, He cried out to God for help; but He did not withdraw from the danger.

After all, where *was* God? Where is God when disaster strikes us? For no apparent reason, some disease begins its wasting process on our bodies or on those of our friends. As in the case of Job, God had declared him to be a righteous man, worthy of His approval; and yet He allowed Job to be cruelly afflicted. He lost his property to bandits; his children were killed by a whirlwind; his body was racked by a loathsome disease; and his so-called friends did their best to extract from him a confession of some hidden wickedness that merited punishment. Even Job's wife offered no support, but urged him to curse God and die.

Or perhaps some sin brings a sudden blot on the character of a family member, plunging the family into embarrassment and disgrace. Why should God allow the innocent to suffer with the guilty person, who is positively hardened and remorseless?

Or it may be that some business reverse reduces a family to abject poverty, and makes them the objects of charity, when they were once prosperous and able to help others.

In any of these circumstances, the ones who suffer are tempted to conclude that God has forsaken them and has left them to bear an intolerable burden without comfort or aid.

During the Second World War, a pastor learned that one of the boys from his church had died on the battlefield. He went immediately to the home of the family to offer what consolation he could. When he rang the doorbell, the father of the family appeared with a crumpled telegram in his hand, and said abruptly to the minister, "Where was God when my son was killed?"

The pastor replied, "Just where He was when His own Son was killed."

God did not intervene by a startling miracle that would have reversed the condemnation of Jesus and blasted His enemies out of existence. He allowed the tragedy to take place because He had a greater answer for it than instant removal. It was necessary that death should be not only defied, but defeated. The victory could not be completed by snatching Jesus from the Cross as His enemies suggested; the overwhelming demonstration of the Resurrection was necessary. Jesus had predicted it and undoubtedly expected it; but to pass through death in expectation of returning gloriously demanded a full and mature faith in the Father who has seemingly forsaken Him. Jesus voiced the feeling that all of us would have were we in His position, and He exhibited the final faith that we should have as He spoke confidently: "Father, into Thy hands I commend My spirit" (Luke 23:46).

Overcoming Through Suffering

God does not exist to spare us all of our griefs. In a world that is racked by violence and poisoned by evil, it is impossible to overcome evil without suffering. It may seem unjust that the innocent should suffer with the guilty, or what is more, that they should suffer when the guilty go unscathed. Yet there emerge from this difficult situation two great principles.

The first is that God is not impassible, or incapable of suffering. Rather He suffers with us. He has felt the pangs of our disappointment and alienation long before we were aware of them. The prophets of Israel uttered the sentiment of God when they wrote of His longing for His people. Hosea, speaking to a nation that had gone over to idolatry and that had rebelled against God's Law, described God's attitude in these words: "How shall I give thee up, Ephraim? How shall I deliver thee, Israel? . . . Mine heart is turned within Me; My compassions are kindled together" (Hosea. 11:8). From the first sin of Eden when man ran away from God who came down to look for him, to the last fugitive who avoids God because he is conscious of his offensive self-will, God feels with people. In the Person of His Son, He has shared human miseries.

A second principle is that He is not defeated by evil. The Cross was an instance of rank injustice. All the meanness, envy, hatred, and brutality of which human nature is capable were exhibited in the treatment accorded to Jesus. To those who loved Him, it seemed to serve no good purpose. Had not innocence been cruelly violated? Had not a career that promised even more than it had accomplished been tragically terminated? Had not the teachings which were so penetrative and so inspiring been invalidated by the patent irony that "He saved others; Himself He cannot save"? (Matt. 27:42) The friends of Jesus were frustrated and bewildered by the Cross, and were unable to reconcile His life with its end. The cynics seemed to have won the day. Yet God had the last word. Out of tragedy, He brought the triumph of Resurrection.

Perhaps the best clue to the mystery is found in the Book of Hebrews: "In the days of His flesh, when He had offered up prayers and supplications with strong crying and tears unto Him that was able to save Him from death . . . though He were a Son, yet learned He obedience by the things which He suffered; and being made perfect, He became the Author of eternal salvation unto all them that obey Him" (Heb. 5:7-9).

God had not left the scene of His suffering, but had permitted the pain, knowing that from it would come the manifestation of the supreme reward for obedience. Jesus was not being punished for anything that He had done; His obedience was being tested to the limit so that He could be the Leader of a redeemed people, bringing many sons unto glory.

In those bitter hours when injustice seems to prevail, when physical suffering becomes unbearable, or when mental and emotional distress threatens to tear apart the human soul, God is standing in the shadows to meet us. As we accept resolutely the test that He permits, He perfects us by its process and brings us out into a richer and more glorious experience. Jesus must have felt the Father's presence as He accepted the Cross, for in the final hour He reverted to addressing God as "Father," and showed that the lifelong intimacy had been only eclipsed, not destroyed.

Out of the agony of that moment came redemption for a world. "For as by one man's disobedience many were made sinners, so by the obedience of One shall many be made righteous" (Rom. 5:19). The absence of God is the last and most painful deprivation that man can undergo, because it takes away his last court of appeal and hope. The realization that God is working through that deprivation to accomplish a greater purpose is sufficient to compensate for the anguish of the moment.

On the wall of my office hangs a small motto that reads:

> There is no gain but by a loss;
> There is no crown without a cross.
> The corn of wheat, to multiply
> Must fall into the ground and die.
> Wherever you ripe fields behold
> Waving to God their sheaves of gold,
> Be sure some corn of wheat has died;
> Some soul has there been crucified;
> Someone has wrestled, wept, and prayed,
> And fought hell's legions undismayed.

The end of the struggle is the victory of God's renewed presence.

12
The Final Test

Jesus saith to Simon Peter, "Simon, son of Jonah, lovest thou Me more than these?"   John 21:15

The men felt bewildered as they trudged along the highway from Jerusalem to Galilee. The events of the preceding days had been exciting, but exhausting. A tragedy had shattered their hopes when Jesus, their leader, had been seized by His enemies, and condemned by their national council. He had then been delivered to the Romans, who had added His execution to the long list of their oppressive acts. The kingdom of which He had spoken had become an illusion as they contemplated His tragic death. In fright they had huddled in an obscure room in Jerusalem behind locked doors, fearing that His enemies would arrest them also. All their hopes which had been set on Him vanished with His death.

Then followed an even more unnerving experience. Three days after His crucifixion, the women of their company reported that the tomb where He had been laid was mysteriously empty. Investigation proved the truth of the women's story, but His body could not be found. Then, as they were discussing this new development, He had appeared to them and identified Himself. They had taken Him for a ghost, but He quickly demonstrated that He was living and present. While they had rejoiced, His reappearance seemed too good to be true. During the following days, there were more appearances. They could not doubt His reality. But their minds were so confused by the mystery of it all that they left the city where these strange things had happened to return to their homes, where they might evaluate them in a less tense atmosphere.

Now they were approaching their home territory. As they mounted the rise that topped the hill south of Capernaum, they could look down on the peaceful lake below. There were the houses of their neighbors, the synagogue where they had worshiped so often in past years and where Jesus had preached, the market in which they had conducted their business, and even the boats they had left to follow Him in His travels.

The events of Jerusalem that brought them sorrow and fright seemed far behind them. It would be easy to settle down again into the old life, and begin once more their usual routine. Jesus, of course, was unforgettable, but He had now passed into another realm from which He appeared only irregularly. The fishing boats presented a rewarding occupation; their families were needing their help; and the past claims and promises were fast fading into memories. Why not resume their old trade and forget their broken dreams?

Simon Peter broke the silence with a declaration of his decision: "I'm going fishing." As if he had spoken what was in their minds, they made the motion unanimous: "We'll go with you." (See John 21:3.)

Before long they had gathered together their nets and had

pulled out from the shore. The cool evening breeze relieved their weariness after the heat of the day, and the activity of fishing turned their attention from their disappointments and doubts. As the night wore on, they were busily engaged with their labors, but their effort was futile. When the early light of dawn broke over the eastern hills, they had nothing to show for their toil.

A Catch of Fish

Just as they were about to accept failure and return to the shore, a voice reached them: "Boys, you haven't caught anything, have you?" Unable to discern the speaker through the misty air, they replied gloomily, "No." Back came the message: "Cast the net on the right side of the boat, and ye shall find."(21:6).

The definiteness of the command must have surprised the disciples. How could a man on the shore tell them, experienced fishermen, where to cast the net? Nevertheless, they had nothing to lose, and possibly something to gain by another attempt, and so they cast the net. The surface of the lake churned as the fish tried to escape, their silver scales flashing in the early sunlight. And the tired men found that they had taken the catch of the season.

Instantly one of them, probably John, though he is not named directly, turned to Peter and said, "It is the Lord!" Memories of an earlier occasion, when under similar circumstances Jesus had provided a catch, flashed into his mind. (See Luke 5:1-14.) Peter, realizing that only the Lord could give them such a return from the lake, dove overboard that he might meet Jesus. The others pulled the boat and its net into the shallow water by the shore.

Knowing that the men were cold and hungry, Jesus had provided warmth and food for them. Around a fire kindled on the beach, they dried their damp clothing and gratefully ate the fish and bread which had been prepared. There could now be no doubt of His identity. The occurrence must have renewed in their memories the occasion when He had summoned them from their ordinary occupations to follow Him. Now that He had risen and manifested His reality to them, there would be a new beginning.

A New Beginning

This new beginning called for a new test. Would these men whose purpose seemed so variable be able to undertake the responsibilities of the opening era? Simon Peter had been the spokesman for the Twelve in the period before the Cross, and was still the recognized leader. His denial was known to all of them, but Jesus had visited him on the Easter morning and had dealt with him personally (Luke 24:34). Now the time had come for an open confession from Peter, which would represent the disciples' dedication, just as his denial had reflected their failure.

When breakfast was over, and as they sat in silence contemplating the miracle of the full net and the reappearance of their Lord, Jesus put a question to Peter.

"Simon, son of Jonah, lovest thou Me more than these?"

How would Simon respond? Jesus used the name that represented the old, rash, hair-trigger, vacillating self that had been replaced by Peter, the stable and substantial rock. Could he and would he live up to Jesus' expectations?

Embarrassed, yet eager to be restored to his place in Jesus' affections and in the esteem of his fellow apostles, Peter said, "Yea, Lord, Thou knowest that I love Thee."

He appealed to Jesus' knowledge of his frequent previous affirmations of loyalty which he had so blatantly denied in the house of the high priest. Surely Jesus must be aware of his genuine appreciation and of his intention to be a worthy disciple, in spite of his lapse. Yet Peter was cautious. He did not trust himself, nor did he dare to promise too much. The word that is used for *love* according to this text is not identical with the one in Jesus' question. While there is room for debate as to whether John were using the synonyms interchangeably as he sometimes did, it would seem strange that he should choose them indifferently in this crucial situation. Jesus' word *agapao* implies a disinterested concern for the welfare of another; Peter's term *phileo* implies family affection and friendship. Whichever interpretation is correct, it indicates Peter's open devotion for Jesus.

Jesus answered with a command: "Feed My lambs." Love brings responsibility. If Peter meant what he said, he should be dealing with living people rather than with dead fish. Jesus' metaphor must have recalled to him the discourse about the sheepfold, given at the Feast of Dedication only a few months before. There Jesus had spoken of those for whom He was about to lay down His life. Redemption made them His choice possession, acquired at indescribable cost. Now He was asking Peter to assume the leadership of these immature followers. Peter himself had been very uncertain in his conduct; could he superintend others?

As he considered this request, Jesus repeated the question: "Simon, son of Jonah, lovest thou Me?" (v. 16)

Peter returned with the same answer: "Yea, Lord, Thou knowest that I love Thee."

Again Jesus commanded him, "Feed My sheep." This time He was speaking of the mature sheep, who needed direction and discipline. It would take all the patience and wisdom that Peter could muster to deal with others who might be as vacillating and emotional as himself.

Then Jesus posed the final question: "Simon, son of Jonah, lovest thou Me?" In this third occasion the verb changes to the one that Peter himself had used. If Peter could not meet Jesus' standard, could Jesus trust him to meet his own? Having failed three times to maintain his loyalty to his Lord, would he be able to demonstrate the love that he now professed?

Peter was grieved because Jesus asked him this question the third time. Was it because Jesus asked it three times, or because on the third occasion Jesus seemed skeptical of Peter's answer? While the lexical argument may not be settled finally, it is certain that Jesus was probing Peter's soul to ascertain whether he were truly sincere and determined to stand fast in his allegiance.

Peter's final affirmation was followed by Jesus' repeated command: "Feed My sheep." He seemed satisfied with Peter's declaration and accepted it at full value.

Three Tests of Love

This threefold test that Jesus applied to Peter is an enlargement of the central principle of the Law of God: "Thou shalt love the Lord thy God with all thine heart, and with all thy soul, and with all thy might" (Deut. 6:5). The proper relation between God and man is that of love, *agape*—as in Jesus' question,—that stands for a voluntary attitude of primary concern for the interests and welfare of another.

God's love for us does not depend on our goodness, for "God commendeth His love toward us in that, while we were yet sinners, Christ died for us" (Rom. 5:8). That love, however, does not mean that He excuses our sins, for they are abhorrent to Him. When we confess and forsake them, He forgives us, and receives us into His family. When Peter professed his love for Jesus, he was not rejected. Jesus took him as he was. Peter's love might be weak, but it was genuine, as was his repentance.

Jesus' questions tested Peter's inner life. Was he still motivated by his old desire for prominence and power, or by a devotion to Jesus' person? Was he willing to humble himself before Jesus, or would he draw back in pride? Was he likely to succumb again to his fears, or would his confidence in Christ enable him to face opposition unflinchingly? Jesus wanted to know Peter's mind before giving him a commission.

The question tested Peter's position in relation to the other disciples. "Lovest thou Me more than these?" has been variously interpreted as relating to the boat, which was his property; or to the fish, which constituted his business; or to the other disciples, his companions. Westcott, in his *Commentary on John*, II, (John Murray, p. 367) takes the last alternative, stating that it is probably a reference to Peter's assertion that whatever the others might do, he would never desert Jesus (John 13:37; Matt.26:33). Since he had professed a greater loyalty than he attributed to the others and had failed, Jesus queried whether he really meant it. Would Peter adhere to his purpose even if the others did not? If he really meant what he said, could Jesus count on him to assume the leadership in the task that awaited them? He was about to commission them to evangelize the world by the message of the resurrection. Would Peter be willing to undergo the sacrifice that the mission would require?

There is always a tendency to make the attitude of the crowd around us our standard for living. We do not want to be different. A workman will not exert himself beyond a certain point; because his associates do not want to work that hard, they would suffer by comparison. A student will be satisfied with mediocrity just to be one of the gang, when he could excel in some field.

Jesus applied a different criterion. He is the One to be satisfied. Love for Him, not conformity to the average, is the chief consideration. The greatness of His love for us provides a new motive: "We love Him, because He first loved us" (1 John 4:19).

The fullness of His forgiveness is an inescapable obligation, because we can never repay by our service the gift of eternal life made available to sinners. The overwhelming consciousness that God has extended undeserved mercy to each one of us eclipses our petty comparisons of ourselves with others. God deals with us individually. He asks for a complete response without wishing to ascertain what the reaction of others may be. The hand of God rules out the jealousies and the disunity that so often disfigure Christian profession and render spiritual efforts powerless. When the imperial persecution of early Christians thrust them into public arenas to be torn to pieces by wild beasts, the stronger always protected the weaker until the very last. The pagans who witnessed their behavior exclaimed in surprise, "See how these Christians love each other!" Their attitude was a more powerful witness than their preaching.

Jesus also tested Peter's attitude toward the future. "When thou wast young, thou girdest thyself, and walkest where thou wouldest; but when thou shalt be old, thou shalt stretch forth thy hands, and another shall gird thee, and carry thee where thou wouldest not" (John 21:18).

Peter had been a very independent young man. His earlier dealings with Jesus revealed his heedless and impetuous nature. He acted first and regretted afterward. Jesus was reminding Peter of his rash urgency to follow Him immediately, when he protested Jesus' unwillingness to consent to it. At that time Jesus had said, "Where I go, thou canst not follow Me now; but thou shalt follow Me afterwards" (John 13:36). Peter was unready for the ultimate crisis, but Jesus predicted it and made it part of His ministry to the world. As it inevitably required the Cross for Him, so would it for Peter, both figuratively and literally.

"Follow Me"

Effectiveness always involves suffering and sacrifice. As a sequel to Peter's threefold declaration of love, Jesus replied, "Follow Me." He summoned Peter to share in the experience of the cross, for He stated that Peter would stretch forth his hands, and would be conducted to his fate against his will. The phraseology was an idiomatic allusion to crucifixion. Jesus Himself had gone that route, and He could promise nothing else to His followers.

Frequently it is harder to live for Christ than to die for Him. The loneliness of being misunderstood, rejected, and ignored, the anguish of enduring the cold sarcasm of unbelievers, the tension of prayer that consumes wakeful hours, and the heavy burden of responsibility for those who need the Gospel and are bitterly opposed to it—all wear down the human spirit. *Following* involves persistence. Nobody ever followed another by standing still while the leader was advancing. The risen Christ asserted that He had a work to do and a goal to attain. If Peter would follow Him, he would emerge from the struggle on the resurrection side.

Roused by this challenge, Peter looked around to see whether any other would share his responsibility. Pointing to John, he said to Jesus, "And what shall this man do?"

Jesus replied, "If I will that he tarry till I come, what is that to thee? Follow thou Me!" (John 21:22) The pronoun *thou* is significant, being seldom used in a command except for emphasis. Jesus was calling Peter directly, and He had to be answered by Peter himself. Peter's concern should not be for the duty of his close friend, but for his own duty. The requirements for Peter would not be relaxed, if those of his associates were less than his. There was and is no way to evade the imperative summons of Christ. If one loves Him supremely, he is bound to serve Him unconditionally

"Till I Come"

What should be the duration of this love? Jesus gave a clue

when He spoke of His return: "Till I come." That would be the next event that would mark the terminus of devotion and labor—not the failure of enthusiasm, but the appearance of the Lord Himself. In one of our popular magazines, there was the account of a new marriage ceremony in which the ordinary vow of fidelity, "as long as we both shall live," was supplanted by "as long as we both shall love." That ceremony substituted emotion for will, inclination for determination. It put transient feeling in the place of a firm and final committal. Such a vow is no vow at all, and is worthless as a reliable foundation for married life. A Christian cannot say that he will love Christ only as long as he feels like it or until some change of circumstance disturbs him. He must focus his attention on the Lord's return, and maintain his first love. As Jesus said to the church of Ephesus, "I have somewhat against thee, because thou hast left thy first love. Remember . . . repent, and do the first works, or else I will come unto thee quickly, and will remove thy lampstand out of its place" (Rev. 2:4-5). The Lord's coming is the objective of our expectations and the final reward of our devotion to Him whom we love and serve.